D1129344

Whole Language Discovery Activities *for the* Primary Grades

Margaret C. Riley
Donna L. Coe

THE CENTER FOR APPLIED
RESEARCH IN EDUCATION
West Nyack, New York 10995

DISCARD
KINSMAN FREE PUBLIC LIBRARY
6420 CHURCH ST.
BOX E
KINSMAN, OHIO 44428
71,520

© 1992 *by*

THE CENTER FOR APPLIED
RESEARCH IN EDUCATION

All rights reserved

Permission is hereby given for individual classroom teachers to reproduce the forms and idea sheets for classroom use. Reproduction of these materials for an entire school system is strictly forbidden.

10 9 8 7 6 5 4 3 2 1

Acknowledgments

The authors would like to thank the following authors and publishers for copyright reprinting permissions: "Helping" and "Hector the Collector," Shel Silverstein, *Where the Sidewalk Ends,* Harper and Row, © 1974; "This Is Halloween," from *Childlife,* © 1941 by Rand McNally Co., used by permission of the author, Dorothy Brown Thompson; "Winter Worlds," *Poetry Place Anthology,* Instructor Books, © 1983, used by permission of the author, Jean Conder Soule; "Dreams" from *The Dream Keeper and Other Poems* by Langston Hughes, © 1932 by Alfred A. Knopf, Inc. and renewed in 1960 by Langston Hughes. Reprinted by permission of Alfred A. Knopf Inc.; "The Pinecone Turkey," "Winter Worlds," "The New Year," "Spring Zing," and "Exercises," *Poetry Place Anthology,* Instructor Books, © 1983; "Magic Penny" words and music by Malvina Reynolds, © 1955, 1959 by Northern Music Company copyright renewed, Rights administered by MCA Music Publishing, A Division of MCA Inc.; "Think-Pair-Share" strategy, Spencer Kagan. Every effort has been made to ensure that no copyrighted material has been used without permission. The authors regret any oversights that may have occurred and would be happy to rectify them in future printings of this book.

Library of Congress Cataloging-in-Publication Data

Riley, Margaret C., 1956–
Whole Language Discovery Activities for the Primary Grades / Margaret C. Riley & Donna L. Coe.
p. cm.
ISBN 0-87628-616-3
1. Reading (Primary)–Language experience approach–Handbooks, manuals, etc. 2. Language arts (Primary)–Handbooks, manuals, etc. 3. Activity programs in education–Handbooks, manuals, etc.
I. Coe, Donna L. II. Title.
LB1525.34.R45 1992
372.6'044–dc20 92–4278
CIP

ISBN 0-87628-616-3

The Center for Applied Research in Education, Professional Publishing
West Nyack, New York 10995
Simon & Schuster, A Paramount Communications Company

Printed in the United States of America

About the Authors

Margie Riley has a B.S. in Elementary Education and an M.S. in Administration/Supervision from George Mason University and has been teaching in Virginia public schools for over 12 years. **Donna Coe** has a B.A. in History from Mary Washington College and an M.Ed. in Elementary Education from University of Virginia and has taught for over eighteen years in four different Virginia public school systems. Margie and Donna met as resource teachers in a primary gifted education program. They have since returned to classroom teaching at the first-grade level. They wrote and published "Crittletivity" (1984–1989), an idea-letter for K–5 teachers based on Torrance's model of creativity. They then compiled their ideas into *Year-Round Creative Thinking Activities for the Primary Classroom,* published by Prentice Hall in 1990.

Using their background in creativity and their natural inclination toward risk-taking, they have enthusiastically embraced the whole-language approach to instruction and learning. They do not consider themselves experts but rather practicing teachers who know the learning and growing characteristics of primary students. They voraciously read professional literature, love working with colleagues, students and parents and consider themselves to be active learners as well as career classroom teachers.

For our families,
the other members of the
Crittletivity staff . . .
with love and thanks.
Donna and Margie

Contents

7 MARCH • 217

8 APRIL • 243

9 MAY • 269

10 JUNE • 295

PERSONAL WORDS FROM THE AUTHORS • 320

Introduction

SCENARIO 1

A classroom teacher has developed enrichment strategies to supplement the basal reading series and is finding that her second graders respond well. Suddenly, she is told she must move away from those methods to develop a literature-based reading program.

SCENARIO 2

An elementary school principal is convinced by current research that students could benefit from teachers implementing a whole language approach to instruction. However, she is also aware of the pattern of today's school systems of putting more and more responsibilities on classroom teachers. She is at odds about how best to approach implementing change.

SCENARIO 3

A first year primary teacher finds himself overwhelmed by the demands on his time and energy. How can he possibly teach reading, writing, math, science, social studies, health, and art and still have any sort of personal life?

SCENARIO 4

An experienced first grade teacher wants to move toward a classroom in which her students are more involved in reading and writing. She has read a lot of informative books and professional articles, but she cannot find an instructional formula. The terms *reading-writing classroom, literature-based reading program, whole language approach,* and *process teaching* are all very confusing to her.

Situations such as these are occurring in schools all over this country. Major questions arise: What is whole language? What is meant by a literature-based reading program? How do you relate skills to children's trade books? What happened to our carefully laid out curricula?

If you've been asking these types of questions, then this book is designed for you. We will not attempt to provide a comprehensive treatment of whole language learning—what we will do, though, is structure strategies and activities around a very basic definition of "whole language" and incorporate the use of Benjamin Bloom's thinking levels.

Whole language, in our opinion, combines research on how children attain language with open, flexible learning opportunities. The teacher structures the classroom environment, schedule, and activities so students discover for themselves the value and personal meaning of our written and oral language. The school day turns to the child's frame of reference and the child's needs and interests. Children are given at-school opportunities to initiate, apply, and enjoy the language skills of reading, writing, speaking, and listening. The teacher models for children a variety of behaviors including reading for meaning and enjoyment, writing as a response or thinking strategy, speaking to share and clarify ideas, and listening for new ideas and thoughts. A variety of literature is the foundation on which student learning is built. Teachers share nonfiction as well as fiction books, songs, poems, letters, journals, movies, picture writing . . . everything that communicates! Through this shared base of information and experience, the teacher can weave curricular concepts and activities to meet different learning objectives.

Benjamin Bloom is an educational researcher who, in the mid-1950s, led a team of researchers at the University of Chicago in developing a taxonomy, or classification, of educational objectives. Bloom's system specifies the types of thinking students exhibit in six levels including knowledge, comprehension, application, analysis, synthesis, and evaluation. The level of student response is directly related to the level of activity or questioning; thus, students benefit most when activities are planned at all levels of Bloom's Taxonomy. We have included activities for each book, poem, and song selection beginning with comprehension/application and moving through analysis, synthesis, and evaluation.

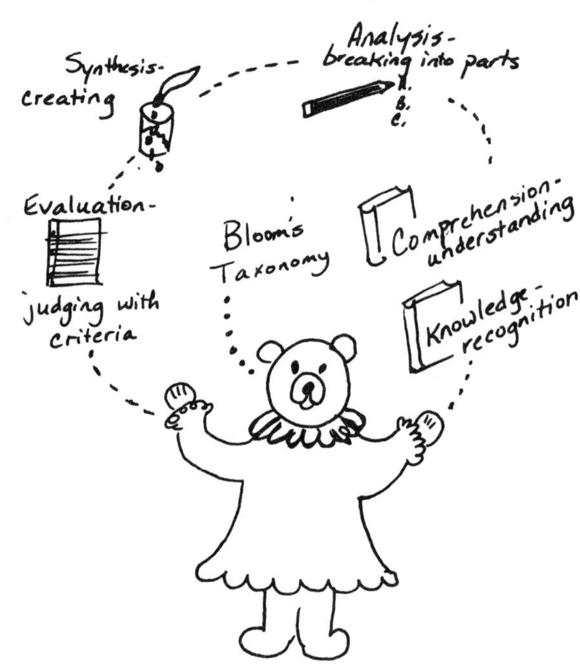

We are happy to note that a whole language approach still uses many of the successful strategies and teaching skills that have been developed through the years. In a whole language classroom, those teaching skills are fine-tuned to fit the perspective of the child. Children are exposed to a variety of literature forms and given a multitude of opportunities to apply, analyze, synthesize, and evaluate that information through language arts, math, science, social studies, health, music, art, and physical education. With inquiry, reflection, and modification, a teacher gradually develops a whole language approach that combines areas of learning in the same way that we find skills naturally combined in real life.

To the Teacher

This book was written to assist teachers in planning integrated lessons that cover many objectives simultaneously. There is no one right way to do this! The essential ingredient of every successful whole language classroom is that children love literature. Teachers must be sensitive to which books are candidates for extension activities and which are best to read to the class, enjoy, and just put back on the bookshelf for individual readers. Teachers must be aware of "teachable moments" sparked by an unexpected but enthusiastic student response and encourage students to share personal connections, observations, and favorite books. Although these conditions often require teachers to abandon carefully planned activities, it is for the greater benefit of students who are actively involved in their own learning . . . and for a whole classroom of students who love reading, writing, speaking, and listening!

Consider the following example:

> A kindergarten class gathers in a circle for the opening exercises. The teacher holds up a bag of shapes and reviews the terms *circle, square, triangle,* and *rectangle* with the class. The students are each given a shape, and as they name their shape they place it on a floor grid to make a class bar graph. When everyone has had a turn, the teacher asks, "What can you tell me about this graph?" The open-ended question encourages children to discover the longest, shortest, and equal rows on their own. The teacher then says, "Watch as our graph becomes a shape pattern train." The teacher takes one shape at a time to create a square-circle-triangle-rectangle train around the perimeter of the graph. The children join in with the teacher's voice as they see the pattern, saying "square-circle-triangle-rectangle, square-circle-triangle-rectangle," etc. Children then have the opportunity to suggest other pattern trains. After reinforcing this pattern building, the teacher shifts the focus by asking, "Would you like to sing a fall song about shapes?" The children chorus "yes!" As the teacher points to an experience chart, the class joins in on words they recognize.
>
> Red and yellow, green and brown,
> All the leaves are falling down.
> Days are crispy, nights are clear,
> Summer's over, autumn's here.

After asking individual children to locate the color words in the song and explain why the song is a "fall" song, the class changes the word *leaves* to *shapes* and sings the song again. At this point, children take a shape and hold it up as their color is sung.

Finally, the teacher shows the class three different pattern sheets of leaves and allows each child to choose which pattern sheet he or she would like to color. Children are encouraged to write the color words for their pattern or write a sentence about their pattern. The pace of the lesson is snappy, and children are active and highly motivated.

Student enjoyment is evident as the teacher is able to integrate the following objectives into the example lesson:

The student will be able to

- listen (language, social studies)
- cooperate, follow directions (language, social studies)
- recognize shapes (math)
- create patterns (math)
- graph, count, compare sets (math)
- recognize that written words have meaning (language)
- identify color words (language)
- identify fall concepts (science)
- write color words, write a sentence (language)
- sing a song (music)

A lot is accomplished in thirty minutes!

Our goal for *Whole Language Discovery Activities for the Primary Grades* is to help classroom teachers, resource teachers, librarians, administrators, and preservice teachers develop strategies and plan activities that actively engage children in language and literature. This book is organized by months of the year to fit the way most teachers view the school year. The literature contained in this book has been chosen according to the following criteria:

- Do children respond enthusiastically to the literature forms?
- Does the work spark extension ideas?
- Is there an overall representational balance of boys and girls, ethnic cultures, realistic and imaginary styles, and content areas?

The activities included have been developed with these points in mind:

- Bloom's Taxonomy and the content areas of language arts, math, science, and social studies are integrated in activities to fit each piece of literature.

- There is a balance of thinking skill levels required of students.
- There are opportunities for reading, writing, speaking, and listening with each work.
- Teachers can easily use one piece of literature all through the school day, in all subject areas.

We've also developed corresponding think-sheets for each chapter. These are not worksheets in the traditional sense, but open-ended response sheets to facilitate recording ideas in individual, small group, and large group activities. Most of the think-sheets and strategies can be easily adapted to fit other pieces of literature. We hope you will enjoy trying, modifying, and extending the ideas to fit your personal favorite books, songs, and poems. Modeling is one of the most important things we do, so enjoy reading, writing, speaking, and listening along with your students.

We hope this resource inspires you to investigate further the whole language approach and to share your findings with colleagues through workshops, grade level meetings, lunch conversations, and careful scrutiny of personal teaching styles. Rediscover the excitement of teaching and learning!

Margaret C. Riley

Donna L. Coe

About This Book

This book is unique because it includes three different forms of literature for each month of the school year. The Caldecott book selections are readily available; the poems and songs have been conveniently printed in full for ready use.

In each monthly section, you will find

- three forms of literature all selected to correspond with monthly themes:
  - –a Caldecott book title with a synopsis
  - –a poem
  - –a traditional song
- language, math, social studies, and science activities developed through the thinking levels of Bloom's Taxonomy for each literature form
- reproducible think-sheets to correspond with specific activities

Additionally, we've included

- an introduction that provides a discussion of whole language and Bloom's Taxonomy
- sections on management and evaluation strategies to assist you in integrating instruction to fit other selections
- a parent section designed to promote home involvement
- a chart correlating the activities with language, math, social studies, and science concepts
- ideas for display

Enjoy selecting, modifying, and extending these teaching ideas as your class integrates forms of literature with required content objectives.

	SKILL CORRELATION CHART	LANGUAGE ARTS	MATH	SOCIAL STUDIES	SCIENCE
SEPTEMBER	*Moja Means One*	Parts of a book: introduction, text, illustrations, pronunciation guide	Number words Skip counting Problem solving Counting	Map skills Continent, Country, Physical features African life	Native animals Coffee beans Artistic technique of using charcoal
	"Helping"	Rhythm Rhyming words	Measuring Problem solving	Jobs	Machines
	"I've Been Working on the Railroad"	Mood	Time	Cooperative work	Sound
OCTOBER	*The Ox-Cart Man*	Story elements: sequence, vocabulary, characterization, mood	Volume Marketing	Production cycles Exchange of goods/ services	Production cycles Materials to products
	"This Is Halloween"	Vocabulary	Comparing sets Rhythm patterns Survey	Neighborhoods	Sounds Five senses Changes Weather
	"She'll Be Coming 'Round the Mountain"	Characters	Sets	Communities	Chain of events

© 1992 by The Center for Applied Research in Education

SKILL CORRELATION CHART		LANGUAGE ARTS	MATH	SOCIAL STUDIES	SCIENCE
NOVEMBER	*Always Room for One More*	Vocabulary	Measurement	Scotland: culture, occupations, geography	Weather
	"The Pinecone Turkey"	Descriptive vocabulary	Geometric shapes	Family traditions	Pinecones
	"Polly Wolly Doodle"	Vocabulary Mood	Map skills Rhythmic patterns	The South	Natural features of the South
DECEMBER	*On Market Street*	Descriptive vocabulary Illustrations	Money Symmetry	Map skills	Classifications Machines Weather
	"Winter Worlds"	Descriptive images Synonyms	Mazes	Geographical areas	Animals
	"This Little Light of Mine"	Metaphors	Classification Sets	Cooperation	Ecology

© 1992 by The Center for Applied Research in Education

	SKILL CORRELATION CHART	LANGUAGE ARTS	MATH	SOCIAL STUDIES	SCIENCE
JANUARY	*Owl Moon*	Characterizations Format Illustrations	Math concepts Time	Families	Owls
	"The New Year"	Cyclical poems and stories	Calendars	Holiday celebrations	Yearly changes
	"If You're Happy and You Know It"	Dramatics	If . . . then logic statements	Feelings	Weather
FEBRUARY	*A Chair for My Mother*	Characterizations	Money Shopping	Families	Volume Five senses
	"Dreams"	Dreams	Number patterns	Brotherhood	Ecology
	"The Magic Penny"	Imagery	Money	Self-concept	Changes

© 1992 by The Center for Applied Research in Education

	SKILL CORRELATION CHART	LANGUAGE ARTS	MATH	SOCIAL STUDIES	SCIENCE
MARCH	*Sylvester and the Magic Pebble*	Story elements	Sets	Safety Feelings	Seasons
	"Windy Words"	Vocabulary	Measurement	Self	Wind
	"Down by the Bay"	Nonsense verse	Problem solving	Geography	Animals
APRIL	*A Tree Is Nice*	Literature about trees	Collecting and using data	Communities	Trees
	"Spring Zing"	Vocabulary	Patterns	Neighborhood	Sound
	"Apples and Bananas"	Long vowel sounds	Measurement	Folk crafts	Nutrition

© 1992 by The Center for Applied Research in Education

	SKILL CORRELATION CHART	LANGUAGE ARTS	MATH	SOCIAL STUDIES	SCIENCE
MAY	*The Girl Who Loved Wild Horses*	Elements of the book	Patterns	American Indians	Hooved animals
	"Exercises"	Following directions	Measurement	Cooperation with partners	Health
	"Over in the Meadow"	Verbs	Counting	Maps	Habitats
JUNE	*Song and Dance Man*	Vocabulary development	Patterns	Memories	Senses
	"Hector the Collector"	Application of the poem	Collection Classification	Cooperation	Recycling
	"Jamaica Farewell"	Calypso music	Measurement: mileage, time, temperature	Jamaica	The sun Seasons

© 1992 by The Center for Applied Research in Education

Classroom Management

"There's so much I want to do!"

"I had this idea months ago and am just *now* getting to it. How am I ever going to manage?"

Perhaps the most important management question a teacher can explore is, "Which strategies will best benefit my class?" The amount of whole language material that's available for classroom use is so overwhelming that a class can't possibly "do" everything, nor would you want it to. The primary strength of the whole language approach is that students are given the tools for learning to learn, which takes them beyond isolated skill acquisition. Using student needs and interests to determine learning strategies differentiates which activities are most useful at a given time. Effective activities result when student needs determine the direction of instruction rather than a "cute" activity formulating the teaching plan. Some ideas must be left aside.

A list of strategies that teachers can use in a variety of situations is given on page 23. These strategies have proven to be effective as generators of activities as well as organizers of information. When strategies are put to use, students easily transfer thinking skills to new situations. Use the checklist on page 23 to plan the use of these strategies in your classroom, and add others that you find effective.

BUDDY TALKS

Purpose: To provide thinking, speaking, and listening opportunities between a student and another person (a peer, older student, parent volunteer, teacher, principal, etc.)

Use: Ask students to have a "buddy talk" after

- reading a selection orally or silently
- taking a field trip
- listening to a guest speaker

	LANGUAGE ARTS	MATH	SOCIAL STUDIES	SCIENCE
BOOKS	Fiction Nonfiction Poetry Music	Books about math skills, mathematicians, solving problems, critical thinking, computers	Books about people, places, present-past-future, solving problems, careers	Books about plants, animals, seasons, weather, nature, ecology, astronomy, nutrition, changes, matter
LIBRARY MATERIALS	Magazines Newspapers Bibliographies Reviews Computer software Posters Television Films, filmstrips, audio and/or video tapes	Computer software Newspapers Charts, tables, graphs Films, filmstrips, audio and/or video tapes Television	Encyclopedias Atlases Biographies Almanacs Films, filmstrips, audio and/or video tapes Magazines	Films, filmstrips, audio and/or video tapes Television Magazines Posters
MANIPULATIVES	Craft supplies Rhythm instruments Music Games Variety of writing materials	Measurement equipment (scales, cooking supplies, rulers, etc.) Patterns Play money Fractional parts Variety of manipulatives Games	Globes, maps Photographs Rhythm instruments Music Craft supplies Codes Artifacts Models	Equipment for experiments Charts Models Artifacts
INTERVIEWS	Letters Tapes of Authors People Surveys Classroom sharing	Letters Mathematicians, people who use math in their jobs Surveys	Letters Historians Sociologists Variety of careers Cultures Surveys	Letters Scientists Surveys

Whole Language Planning Chart

- viewing a film, tape, or television program
- watching a presentation
- ____________________
- ____________________

Either assign buddies or ask students to pair up with a person sitting near them. (Buddy talks may involve a group of three students, too.) Pose a question to focus their "talk." After a few minutes' discussion time, ask the partners to share what each other said. This sharing might be done with the whole group, with another pair of buddies, or in a written form. (See the sample shown here.)

Buddy Talk

Today I talked with ________

about ________________

Signature | Buddy's signature | date

Example: The class has just listened to *A Chair for My Mother* by Vera B. Williams (see February), and you would like a quick comprehension check. Ask students to share with their buddies their analysis of the main action and the outcome. Then ask students to tell a personal connection to the story predicament with their buddy.

Advantages: Buddy talks allow many children to speak simultaneously and satisfy their need to share ideas. Shy children, as well as verbal children, share thoughts through the one-on-one format.

LISTEN-THINK-PAIR-SHARE

Purpose: This strategy, developed by Spencer Kagan, is effective for involving all students in a whole-group discussion. Students enjoy the pattern of thinking and responding, and it gives all students a chance to verify their responses in advance.

Use: Following the presentation of new information (a reading selection, a guest speaker, etc.), ask students to *listen.* State a question about the material once. Ask students to sit quietly for fifteen seconds and *think.* Then ask students to *pair* up with a designated person and discuss their thoughts about the question. Finally, provide students time to *share* their ideas by telling the group their partner's answer.

Example: The class has just listened to the poem "This Is Halloween" (see October). You are interested in how well the class understands vocabulary from the poem. Turn a pointer on a listen-think-pair-share chart to *listen.* Ask, "What do you think a fate-cake is?" Then turn the chart to *think,* and the class thinks quietly. When you turn the chart to *pair,* students turn to one another, buzzing about their ideas of fate-cakes. Switch the chart to *share,* and give students a chance to tell the whole group what their partner's ideas were. The same procedure could be followed for other vocabulary phrases in the poem or for the question, "What Halloween things would you combine in a poem like this, and why?"

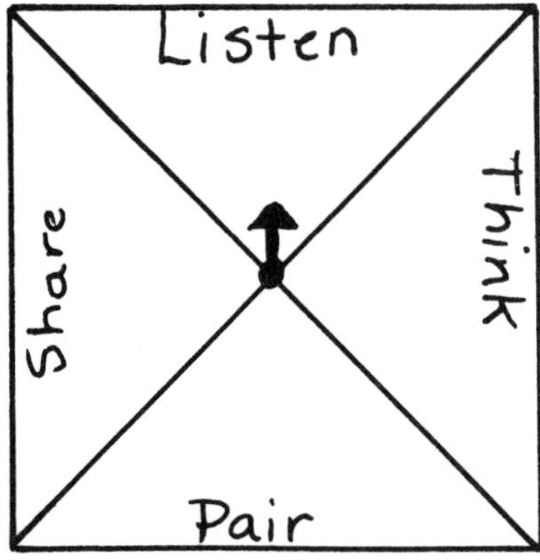

Advantages: The direct approach of this strategy emphasizes student thinking time and sharing time. It's highly motivating and keeps the pace of a discussion snappy.

K-W-L

Purpose: K (what we know), W (what we want to find out), and L (what we learned) is a three-step procedure for focusing the direction instruction will take in a particular topic of study.

Use: K-W-L assists students in activating prior knowledge when approaching a new subject. It helps them focus their research for specific information. It provides a stimulus for discussion. It provides a visual documentation of what has been learned through a unit of study.

Suggestion: For visual interest, put the chart on a shape that corresponds to the topic of discussion. See the following example on wild horses.

K.W.L.

______________ date

Today we did a "KWL" about

____

Ask me what I knew, what I wanted to find out, and what I learned!

______________ signature

Step 1 – Brainstorm with the students everything they already know about the key concept of the planned study.

Step 2 – List questions students pose of things they would like to find out about the topic.

Step 3 – Read! Research!

Step 4 – Chart information that answers questions, and target unanswered questions for further research. Ask for any additional questions the reading may have prompted.

Step 5 – Further reading!

Example: Wild Horses

Advantages: This strategy activates students' prior knowledge and creates a connection between resources they've already explored and the new information. K-W-L saves time! The familiar material can be reviewed quickly, and greater emphasis can be placed on new learning. All students are pulled into the thinking process, thereby cementing the new learning.

SHOULDER TAP RESEARCH

Purpose: This method of research allows a class to move independently through the fact-finding stage of research.

Use: A collection space is designated in the classroom for facts about the current topic. One person starts the research by going to the library and writing down one fact about the topic. Upon returning to the classroom, he or she posts that fact in the collection space and quietly taps another student on the shoulder. The second student silently reads the first fact and goes to the library to find a second fact, different from the first, to post. Each successive student taps another student, who reads the collection of facts before finding a new one at the library. When all students have had a turn, the many different facts are read aloud and used for a group or independent writing activity.

Example: Second graders want to find out more about trains after singing the song "I've Been Working on the Railroad" (see September). One child begins the chain of research by finding a fact from the *T* encyclopedia volume in the library and posting it on a bulletin board in the classroom. Students continue the research as their shoulders are tapped. Finally, the whole group compiles the facts into a class book about trains.

Advantages: Students build independence as they read collected facts, research the topic at the library, and add new facts to a display. Finding one new fact is not an overwhelming assignment, and the shoulder tap is highly motivating. The strategy is self-managing; once begun, you can continue with other activities as children send themselves one by one to the library.

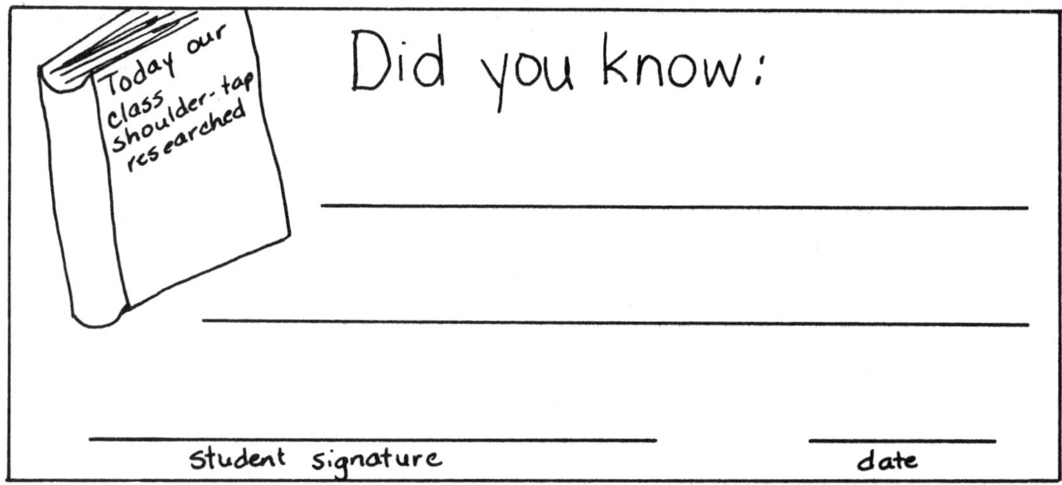

SHARING-RESPONSE STRATEGIES

Purpose: Sharing-response strategies are follow-ups to reading, writing, speaking, and listening activities. These strategies involve students in immediately thinking about the given material and increase motivation.

Use: Be sure to model the thinking and writing processes the first time students are involved in one of these strategies and then provide students with a practice opportunity. List the strategy on a class chart once it's been introduced. Students can then choose which strategy they would like to use in response to a given activity.

Note: A specialized blank response sheet follows each language selection in this book. These are well suited for recording ideas generated by the following strategies:

1. *Five W's and an H!* Students write *who* was in the selection, *what* the main action was, *when* it occurred, *where* it occurred, *why* they liked or didn't like the selection, and *how* they might put the selection to use. (It was enjoyable, there was factual information that will be helpful for ______, they could refer a friend interested in the topic, etc.)

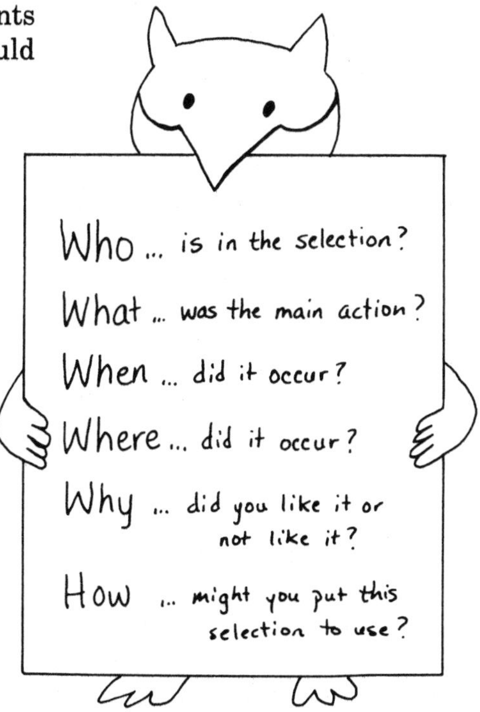

2. *Letters to the author, illustrator, characters, editor, inanimate objects in the story, etc.* Students write a letter to one of the above, summarizing the material, giving their opinion about the selection, or asking any questions they may have. If the letter is to the author or illustrator, consider sending it. If it's addressed to a character, perhaps someone in the class would answer the student's letter from the character's point of view.

3. *Story map.* Story maps come in a variety of forms. Judge the amount of detail to be included in the story map by students' needs. A minimum amount might be the story characters, main action, outcome, and author's purpose. More involved detail includes setting, time, sequence, supporting details, inferences, and conclusions.

My Story Map

Characters	Main Action	Outcome

Story Map

Characters:
Setting:
Time:

Sequence:

Outcome:
Inferences:

4. *Venn diagram.* Students compare books, illustrations, places, holidays, people, characters, etc. They list similarities in the middle of the Venn diagram and differences on each side.

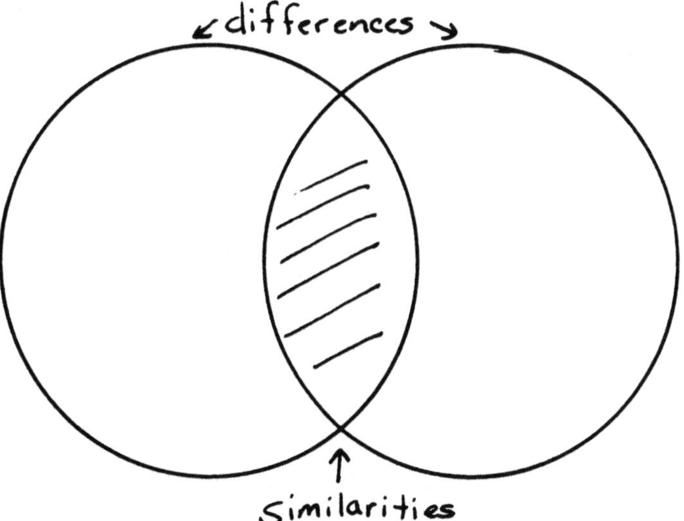

5. *Letter of recommendation.* Students write a letter summarizing the highlights of the selection, giving reasons why it's one to recommend or not, and stating who, if anyone, might find it enjoyable.

6. *Alternate ending.* Students pose one or more alternate endings to the selection. They should be ready to support their ideas.

And then ....

7. *If I were . . .* Students take the point of view of an author, illustrator, editor, or character and tell why this selection is important to them.

If I were...

8. *If I could have a part in the . . .* Students consider if they were a part of the selection. Where would they fit in? What needs to be added if they become part of the story? What could be eliminated? What other changes might occur? Students must explain their thinking.

If I could have a part in the ________________, ...

STRATEGIES CHECKLIST

STRATEGY	DATES USED
Buddy Talks	
Listen-Think-Pair-Share	
K-W-L	
Shoulder Tap Research	
Sharing-Response Strategies*:	
Five W's and an H	
Letters to ____	
Story Map	
Venn Diagram	
Letter of Recommendation	
Alternate Ending	
"If I Were . . ."	
"If I Could Have . . ."	
Others:	

*These may be oral or written activities.

© 1992 by The Center for Applied Research in Education

Evaluation

The whole language approach to literacy frees us to enjoy students and their learning through planning classroom experiences that address student needs and interests. The evaluation process, in keeping with the overall philosophy, also centers on student growth, needs, and interests.

Keeping in mind that evaluation should

- provide information for instructional planning,
- help analyze each child's growth,
- allow us to analyze our own teaching,
- provide a base for communications with parents and administrators, and
- aid the student in evaluating his or her own growth,

we constantly observe student attitudes, abilities, and interests. We use both formal and informal ongoing assessment tools and focus on what the child *can do*. Formal assessment tools include tests, final drafts, and portfolios. Informal assessment tools include anecdotal records, checklists, learning logs, conferences, and dated work samples.

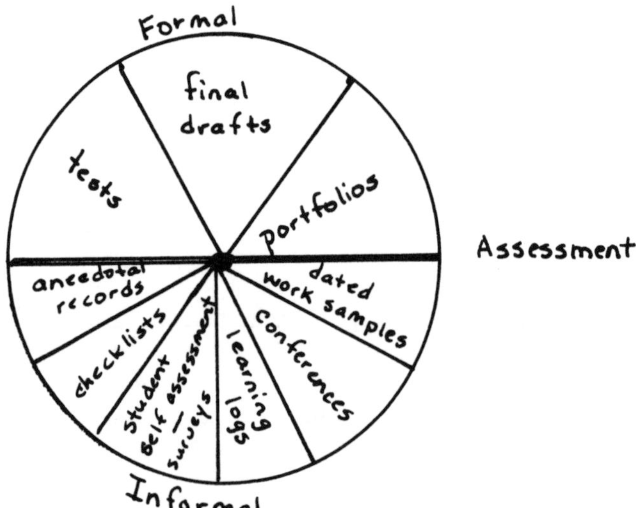

By working with materials that are relevant to the students and asking open-ended, higher-level questions, we have boundless opportunities to observe student understanding. The student joins us in the assessment process through periodic conferencing and is kept abreast of what skills and abilities he or she is using effectively and what skills or thinking need further development. This multidimensional evaluation assesses processes as well as products, thereby enabling us, parents, administrators, and students to see instructional needs and student growth.

Skills are still measured, but they are presented at the time students have an authentic reason to use them. The curriculum becomes more effective as it reflects true student learning needs rather than a predetermined sequence of skills.

Examples of different types of informal assessment strategies are included in the following pages. They provide a baseline plan for evaluation: as always, we adapt strategies to fit particular needs of specific situations.

ANECDOTAL OBSERVATIONS

Teachers gather data by making continuous observations throughout the day. We jot down phrases for students that document oral language development, reading proficiency, writing development, interest areas, task commitment, and social behavior. These dated notes can help with planning for individual needs and serve as an excellent resource for writing formal evaluations. See the sample forms on pages 26–29.

Keeping anecdotal records is a personal and illuminating evaluation method. Teachers' record-keeping strategies vary according to individual preferences. Some forms that anecdotal observations can take include

- designating a page for each student in a small spiral notebook
- making notations on self-stick notes and collecting them in individual student work sample folders
- using forms to make daily or weekly notations for the whole class (a clipboard is useful!)
- having students keep notebooks in which teachers and students record observations
- maintaining a file card box of teacher and student observations

Developing a "shorthand" code is useful in recording observations in the midst of instruction. This saves writing time and provides data at a glance.

Example: B – beginning a writing
R – revising a writing
C – conference
P – publishing
* – working with a partner
ab– absent

ANECDOTAL RECORD
(Individual)

Name ______________________________

DATE	OBSERVATIONS

© 1992 by The Center for Applied Research in Education

ANECDOTAL RECORD (Class)		WEEK OF:
Name:	Name:	Name:
Name:	Name:	Name:
Name:	Name:	Name:
Name:	Name:	Name:
Name:	Name:	Name:
Name:	Name:	Name:
Name:	Name:	Name:

© 1992 by The Center for Applied Research in Education

ANECDOTAL RECORDS
(Class)

Week of: ______________________

STUDENTS	MON.	TUES.	WED.	THURS.	FRI.

© 1992 by The Center for Applied Research in Education

READING/WRITING RECORD (Individual)

Name: ____________________

NOTES (topics, titles, sharing/conference partners)

	MON.	TUES.	WED.	THURS.	FRI.
WRITING: Draft/Revision					
Conference					
Sharing					
Extension					
Other					
READING: Conference					
Assigned/Self-Selected					
Group/Individual					
Extension					
Other					

© 1992 by The Center for Applied Research in Education

CHECKLISTS

Checklists record student performance on specific tasks. They provide a quick visual summary of class performance and facilitate forming small instructional groups.

Checklists ensure that students have been taught essential skills. In this way, checklists are a valuable instructional planning tool. Further, they provide useful information for parent-teacher conferences, reports to administrators, student self-assessments, and report cards.

Once again, inventing codes can maximize the usefulness of the checklist. For example,

✓= satisfactory performance
+= excellent performance
O= incomplete
⊕= incomplete, but the work that was done was excellent
ab= absent

Many literacy assessment checklists are widely available, but the most useful ones will be those you develop to suit your own instruction program, teaching style, and documentation requirements. A few sample checklists are provided on pages 31–33 as a starting point for this process.

STUDENT LOGS

Student logs provide the student an opportunity to write a response to a literature selection or learning activity. Pose questions for students to respond to, or students may choose their own written response idea. An evaluation of the student's writing indicates the thinking level of his or her response, the student's ability to communicate effectively in writing, and his or her personal interest in the activity. We can quickly surmise whether the student has been working on a knowledge/comprehension level of thinking or whether the student is reaching levels of application, analysis, synthesis, and evaluation.

Examples of response log questions include

- If I were in the main character's shoes . . .
- As I was reading, I began to think of . . .
- This is like . . .
- It would be ________ if this happened *(change the setting, time, or a character)* because . . .
- I know the feeling . . .
- Key words for this selection include . . .

CHECKLIST (class)

READING

	STUDENTS' NAMES																	
ATTITUDES	Enjoys books																	
	Uses the library																	
	Selects different kinds of books																	
	Participates actively in shared book experiences																	
	Talks about books in informal conversations																	
COMPREHENSION	Can retell story																	
	Demonstrates understanding of:																	
	plot																	
	main idea																	
	setting																	
	characters																	
	Reads fluently																	
	Reads with expression																	
	Makes personal connections																	
	Identifies supporting details																	
	Compares with other selections																	
STRATEGIES	Reads for meaning																	
	Makes predictions																	
	Self-corrects errors																	
	Uses prior knowledge																	
	Figures out vocabulary using:																	
	context																	
	picture clues																	
	phonics																	
	help from another person																	

© 1992 by The Center for Applied Research in Education

CHECKLIST (class)

WRITING — STUDENTS' NAMES																		
Participates in group writing activities																		
Revises ideas																		
Illustrates text																		
Can read back writings																		
Uses invented spellings																		
Self-selects topics for writing																		
Uses writing to communicate ideas																		
Includes opinions/feelings in writings																		
Shows awareness of audience																		
Shares own writing																		
Uses correct grammar																		
Uses complete sentences																		
Uses punctuation correctly																		
ORAL LANGUAGE/LISTENING																		
Demonstrates good listening skills																		
Uses clear oral language																		
Works cooperatively with others																		
Displays confidence in sharing																		

CHECKLIST
(individual)

Name ______________________________

Book title ______________________________

Author ______________________________

Date started ______________ Date completed ______________

	EXCELLENT	SATISFACTORY	NEEDS IMPROVEMENT
READING			
WRITING			
DISCUSSION			
COMMENTS Student: Teacher: Parent:			

- My quickest comment about this selection is . . .
- I think the author . . .
- What if . . .
- I can't believe . . .
- I never thought about . . .
- __________ reminds me of . . .
- I really can't understand . . .
- I was surprised . . .
- I noticed . . .
- As a summary of this, I would say . . .
- I liked . . .
- I disliked . . .
- My prediction for what might happen next is __________, because . . .
- A question I would ask about this is . . .
- I think the reason the author wrote this is . . .

Alternate Idea: Write response cues on character shapes, and pass to students for oral discussion of a reading or writing activity.

CONFERENCES

Conferences provide a valuable opportunity for two-way communication about reading, writing, speaking, and listening. They may be set up to involve the whole class, small groups, or individuals. The amount of teacher involvement can range from teacher directed to peer directed, with all kinds of variations within these parameters.

The main objectives of a conference are to provide the reader/writer with information to consider for the next step (self-evaluation), to provide other students with opportunities to evaluate and support the efforts of a peer, and to provide important information about the growth of all students involved in the process. Some questions that can help focus the conference and develop the students' responsibility for their own learning are:

- What do you feel you learned in this reading/writing?
- What can you do well in reading/writing?
- What do you want to learn next in order to improve your reading/writing?
- How will you go about learning that?

In the beginning, we must carefully model and reinforce appropriate, supportive responses. We must encourage the student who is sharing to trust the classroom community to be an effective sounding board and convince all students to be worthy of that trust. As students practice these behaviors, they are eager to assume more and more responsibility in the give-and-take of reading and writing conferences.

Many books and articles have been written about how to facilitate effective conferences. It is helpful to be familiar with the variety of resources while keeping in mind that there is no one right way to conduct conferences. Once again, student needs and interests and your teaching style should determine the conferencing process for your classroom. Further, varying the conference process from time to time can capture and maintain student interest throughout the school year. Some ideas for structuring conferences include those on pages 36–38.

RESPONSE ROLES

Assign specific roles to listeners. After the reader/writer shares, the . . .

. . . "complimenter" acknowledges a strength

Examples: "You read that book with good expression."
"I like how scary your story is!"

READING—CONFERENCE RECORD
(individual)

Student's name ______________________________

BOOK TITLE	DATE OF CONFERENCE	COMMENTS

WRITING—CONFERENCE RECORD
(individual)

Student's name ______________________

DATE	WRITING ACTIVITY, CONFERENCE NOTES, ETC.

WRITING—CONFERENCE RECORD
(class)

Week of: ______________________

Code: D = drafting
R = revising
S = sharing
C = conferencing
P = publishing

STUDENTS' NAMES	MON.	TUES.	WED.	THURS.	FRI.

© 1992 by The Center for Applied Research in Education

. . . "questioner" asks a clarifying question

Examples: "How did you figure out that tricky word ________?"

"Why do you have the character of your story do ________?"

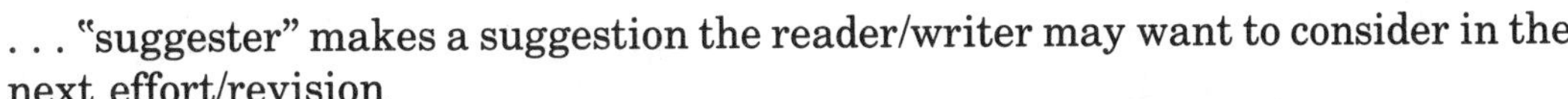

. . . "suggester" makes a suggestion the reader/writer may want to consider in the next effort/revision

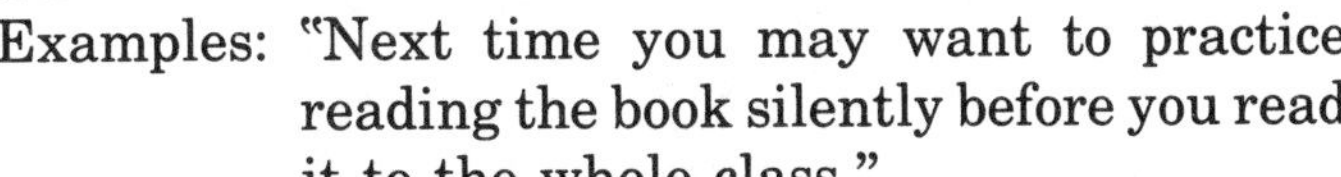

Examples: "Next time you may want to practice reading the book silently before you read it to the whole class."

"I'd like to hear more details about ______________."

These assigned roles can be written on index cards or headbands to help students remember the points of view they are to assume. These visual aides also serve as a badge of importance to the participants. Teaching students to thank each other for compliments, questions, and suggestions helps maintain the trusting classroom environment and thus promotes the desired risk taking which is so essential for growth in reading and writing.

SELF-STICK NOTES

Write constructive student responses to reading/writing on self-stick notes and place them on the student's folder. (Students may be able to write their own comments on the self-stick notes–so much the better!) This allows the student who is sharing to relax during the conference and to consider the comments carefully at a later time. It also provides the student with collections of supportive statements about his or her work. What could be more of a boost to self-esteem!

RATE THE SPEAKER

In oral sharing (such as conferences, reports, and show-and-tell), have students rate the effectiveness of the speaking from the audience's point of view. A simple rating slip could be used, which is then given to the speaker.

_______________ shared today and

remembered to:

- ☐ speak loudly enough
- ☐ speak clearly
- ☐ hold items in sight (book, poster, etc.)
- ☐ stand still
- ☐ look at audience

Signed: Date:

GOOD LISTENER COUPONS

After receiving constructive comments and questions about reading/writing, the sharing student could distribute "good listener" coupons to students who demonstrated especially good listening manners during the conference.

Provide an additional incentive by allowing students who receive a specific number of these coupons an extra playtime or other reward.

RECORD KEEPING

The simpler the record-keeping system, the more likely it will be maintained throughout the school year. Clipboards, small notebooks, and self-stick notes have all proven to be useful tools in documenting student reading/writing conferences. The main purpose of this record-keeping is to ensure that all students have opportunities to participate actively in scheduled conferences. Document this information with individual or whole class notations. Whenever possible, have students maintain their own charts; add observations when appropriate. This can save time and demystify the evaluation process. Sample charts for this purpose are included on pages 31–33 as a starting point for developing an evaluation system.

Parent Materials

Research consistently shows that parental involvement in school is a strong predictor of student success. When parents read to their child an hour per day, the child comes to school with over 1,500 hours of exposure to literary language. Continued parental interest provides support to the child's efforts and enhances school learning.

Forming a partnership with parents is an important aspect of the total teaching picture. While some parents are quite adept at providing natural learning experiences at home, others are unsure about what to do to help their child. They may fear doing something wrong, or they may consider themselves unqualified to give their child assistance. For these reasons, parents are more likely to use specific suggestions instead of broad, generalized ideas. This section includes a beginning list of specific ideas to involve parents in their child's education. Expand and adapt these ideas to suit student needs, teaching styles, and parent volunteer programs.

BEGINNING-OF-THE-YEAR PARENT LETTER

This is one of the most important communications of the year. (See page 44.) Consider sending it before school starts along with a "Welcome to ________ grade" note for the student.

REQUEST PARENT INPUT

Send home the interest inventory (see page 45) during the first weeks of school. Parental input regarding student interests can provide highly motivational springboards for the classroom. Tally the ideas and use the information to pair students by interests or plan special topic investigations.

PARENT GUEST READERS

Throughout the year, spark interest in reading by inviting parents to school to share their favorite children's book with the class. (See the notes on page 46.) Take a "book break" at whatever time the guest reader is able to visit your classroom. The spontaneity is part of the fun!

Send the letter home or have students write invitations themselves. The parent reply form could be enclosed in the student invitation.

Consider having the students make thank-you notes that could be signed quickly and sent home on the day of the visit.

If the children respond enthusiastically to the story, consider developing some follow-up activities for the story using any of the strategies suggested in the Classroom Management section, or pattern an activity after one of the many ideas in the monthly chapters.

HELPFUL AT-HOME ACTIVITIES

Use the idea list beginning on page 47 to give parents specific ideas to promote language development at home. Add ideas that reflect specific student needs.

WEEKLY READING LOG

Promote reading at home by encouraging the use of the reading log (see page 48). Provide time at school for students to share their logs.

WEEKLY NEWSLETTER

At the close of each day, ask students to dictate a sentence about their listening, speaking, writing, and reading activities (see page 49). At the end of the week, send the newsletter home for parents.

POTPOURRI OF IDEAS

Use the idea sheet on page 50 as a follow-up during the school year.

PLANNING SHEET FOR PARENT COFFEE NIGHT

The planning sheet on page 51 will help plan and manage a successful parents' night.

WHOLE LANGUAGE CHART

Use the chart on page 14 as a planning tool to help integrate whole language across the curriculum and to maintain student interest through a variety of resources. Space is available for additional ideas.

Dear Parents,

I am delighted to have the opportunity to work with your child and with you during this new school year. There is so much to learn and discover and practice—I can't wait to get started!

This letter is to provide you with an overview of the ____ grade instructional program. Based on research and teaching experience, I am planning a developmentally sound literacy program for the children in Room ____. Every day your child will be learning by

- reading books, poems, songs, and other writings
- listening to quality children's literature, teacher-directed lessons, and ideas generated in classroom discussions and sharing
- writing stories, messages, thoughts, responses
- speaking in large and small group discussions

Each of these areas strengthens the others! The more your child becomes involved in reading, listening, writing, and speaking, the more confidence and competence he or she will develop. Science, social studies, health, math, and language arts are all integrated so that instruction is in line with how young children naturally learn. This is called the whole language approach to literacy.

There are several things you can do at home to support your child's learning. The most important thing is to read to your child every day, even after he or she reads independently. Do not try to "teach" reading skills—just read and enjoy and discuss interesting aspects of the book. Another thing you can do is to encourage your child to write using "invented" spelling. Research has shown that children who employ invented spellings become more relaxed and competent spellers than those children who only write words they know how to spell correctly.

Surround your child with reading and writing materials. Celebrate your child's efforts. Enjoy literature together. You will both be amazed at the results!

I value our partnership and look forward to working with you this year. Please do not hesitate to call me if you have any questions.

Sincerely,

____

Teacher

© 1992 by The Center for Applied Research in Education

Beginning-of-the-Year Letter to Parents

Dear Parents,

I am interested in knowing more about your child's interests so that I can build on them as I plan classroom activities throughout the year. Please help me by providing any of the following information:

My child shows a great deal of interest in:

My child's favorite play activities:

My child's favorite books:

My child's favorite songs/poems:

Other activities we enjoy together at home:

Places my child has enjoyed visiting:

Other notes of special interest about my child:

Thank you for your help! Please feel free to share this kind of information with me at any time during the year.

Sincerely,

____

Teacher

Interest Inventory

© 1992 by The Center for Applied Research in Education

Dear Parents,

____
(date)

Our ____________ graders love being read to! Could you join us during the day, at your convenience, to share your favorite children's book with the class? If so, please fill out the following information and return it to school. I'll contact you to verify a time.

Thank you for volunteering!

____
Teacher

____ Yes, I'd like to be a guest reader. The book I'd like to share is

____

____

Convenient times for me to visit include ____________________________________

____

____
Parent

Guest Reader Invitation

© 1992 by The Center for Applied Research in Education

____
(date)

Dear __________________________,

Thank you for volunteering time to be a guest reader in our classroom! We look forward to seeing you

____________________________________ at ____________________________________.
(date) (time)

Please come right into the classroom, as I will keep the children working until you arrive. We will then gather for your favorite book. Thanks again!

____
Teacher

Guest Reader Thank You and Time Verification

Ideas for Home!

"What can we do?" "Here's an idea!"

☐ **Read Together Often.** Set a specific time as part of a routine, or read spontaneously whenever the opportunity arises. Just be sure book-sharing averages out to a good half hour each day. After reading together, talk about the book using *one* of the following ideas:

- talk about the parts you each enjoyed most
- discuss the characters, their problem, and the outcome of the story
- talk about the illustrations or other interesting features of the book
- tell any personal stories you have that might relate to the book

☐ **Ask Your Child for a School "News Report."**

- What did you read at school today?
- What did the teacher read to the class?
- Did anyone else work with the class?
- Was there an activity that was especially fun?

Respond to your child's report with a specific comment. For example, "That book about monsters is a good one for October because of Halloween." Or, "I like animals, too. Don't we have a book about bears here at home?"

☐ **Think About Oral Language.**

- Sing songs together in the car . . . in the tub . . . while dressing . . . while playing . . . and so on.
- Make up your own words to a familiar tune. For example, "Are You Sleeping?"

Let's go shopping,
We need some groceries.
Put on your coat.
Put on your hat!

- Have conversations with your child. Use precise words. For example, instead of saying, "Let's pick up the toys," say "Let's pick up the blocks and the stuffed animals."
- Talk about interesting things that happened during the day. For example, "I noticed a chickadee watching me while I was in the yard."
- Discuss favorite television shows. For example, "That reminds me of the time we watched ________." Or, "Remember when we did something like that?"
- Build vocabulary by using specific words. For example, "I need a claw hammer to drive this nail into the wall" is better than saying "I need a tool."

☐ **Take Advantage of New Sights and Experiences.** When you're traveling, have everyone take turns pointing out interesting things to notice, or keep a family journal of the trip. Compare/contrast the new experience to a familiar one. (This part is like ________ because ________. It's different because ________.)

© 1992 by The Center for Applied Research in Education

Name ______________________ Date ______________________

PARENTS: As you enjoy reading with your child this week, have your child list the subjects or book titles. Dictated responses, pictures, and invented spelling are welcome. Send this to school on Friday for a sharing time. Thank you!

This week, we read books about:

I would recommend the following book to a friend: ______________________

because ______________________

© 1992 by The Center for Applied Research in Education

Reading Log Invitation

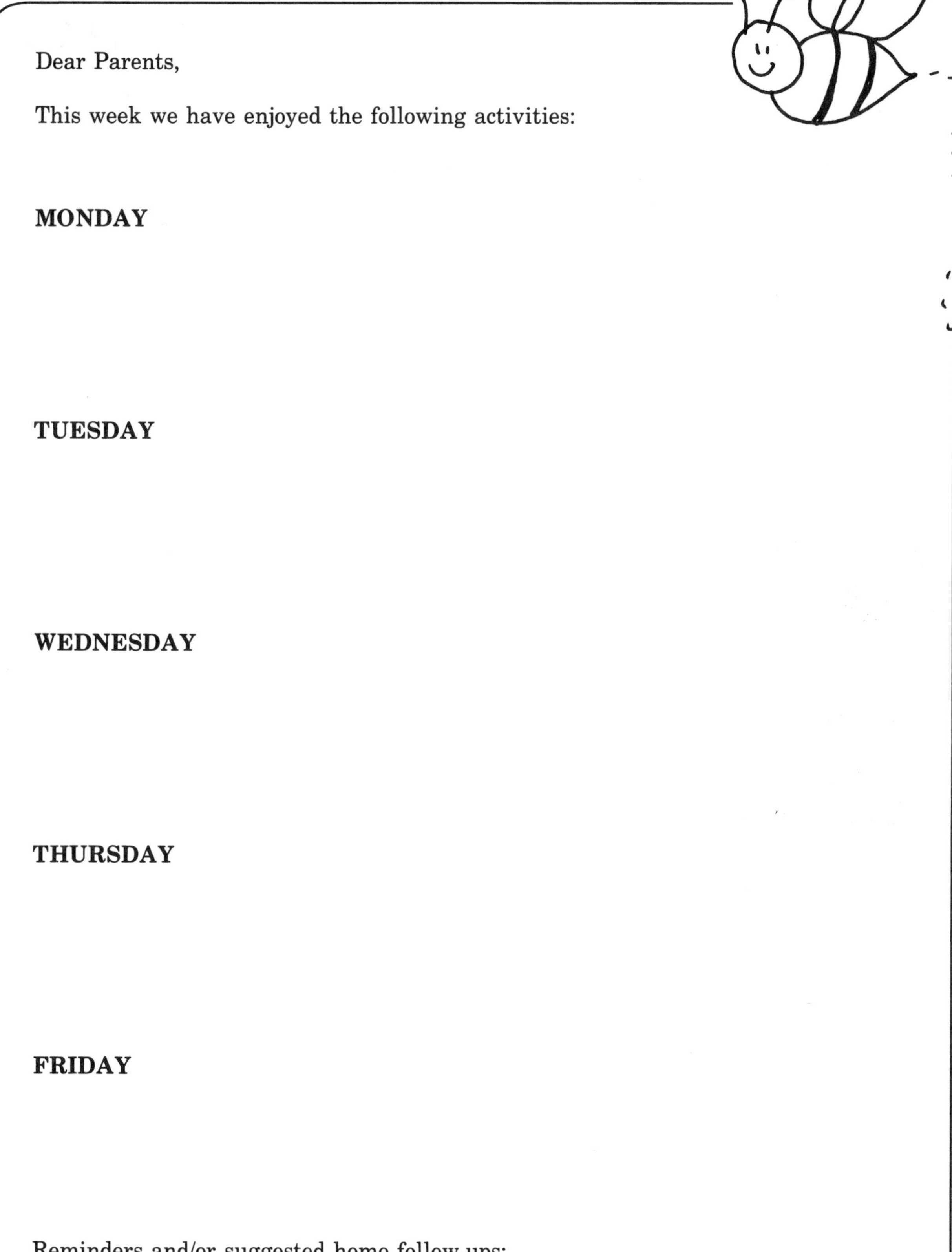

Dear Parents,

This week we have enjoyed the following activities:

MONDAY

TUESDAY

WEDNESDAY

THURSDAY

FRIDAY

Reminders and/or suggested home follow-ups:

© 1992 by The Center for Applied Research in Education

Weekly Newsletter

NEED SOME NEW
AT-HOME READING IDEAS? TRY THESE!

- Read together directions to all sorts of things: recipes, packaged mixes, medicines, shampoo bottles, games, laundry items, etc.
- Write notes back and forth with your child on a message board.
- Leave notes for your child to find – next to the toothpaste, under his or her pillow, in his or her pocket, etc.
- As you enjoy books together, pause at an opportune time in a sentence and let your child fill in the word. Or, deliberately make mistakes and encourage your child to catch you.
- Use checklists for daily tasks. Have your child check off the accomplished items.
- Make labeling photographs a family project. Have your child write in captions or compose photo book summaries.
- Find several books at the library that are about the same animal as your family pet. Compare the stories with your pet's actions.
- Write to grandparents asking them for their favorite childhood book memories. Read any books they recommend.
- ____
- ____

© 1992 by The Center for Applied Research in Education

Potpourri of Ideas List

Parent Night Plans

Topic:

Announcements sent:

Outline of information I plan to share:

Handout materials for parents:

Display items:

Other arrangements:

space

refreshments

notify custodian

invite other staff members

audiovisual equipment needed

Planning Sheet for Parent Coffee Night

© 1992 by The Center for Applied Research in Education

Bulletin Board Display Ideas

Bulletin boards are an integral part of the school environment. When used to display children's work, they promote self-esteem and intrinsic pride in accomplishments. Within the context of whole language learning, the bulletin board can be a liaison between the dynamics of the classroom and the observer walking by, showing that daily work reflects student learning.

Here are a few suggestions regarding optimum use of bulletin boards:

- When displaying children's work, include a brief summary of the idea and classroom thinking that generated the products. The open-ended idea sheets accompanying each book, poem, and song section are useful for recording and displaying this summary.
- Throughout the school year, vary the products displayed: writings, artwork, charts, maps, puppets, and so on. Be sure to include the book title, poem, or song in the display, too.
- Consider displaying "draft" work to show how the learning process takes students through several stages. Label the display "drafts," add a "to be continued" sign, and then post final products when an idea is complete.
- Use sentence strips and bubble clouds that students have dictated to highlight titles and idea summaries. They're an efficient means of conveying main ideas and ensuring student ownership of the display.
- Use three-dimensional materials with displays to heighten interest.
- Capitalize on a speciality of the literature or song selection to add spark to displays. For example, use an artistic aspect of the story in your display. *Moja Means One* is particularly suited to charcoal letters. In a response to *A Tree is Nice,* the class could watercolor a large mural of trees for the background of the display.

- Include both student and teacher involvement in the bulletin board.
- Bulletin boards could connect to a central idea or theme of the selection. For the song "I've Been Working on the Railroad," students' work could be displayed as train cars. Daily work for *On Market Street* would catch the reader's eye by being displayed on a backdrop of a market street vendor's stall.

- The border of the bulletin board could also carry the theme of a selection. A border of students' hands cut out of construction paper would be appropriate for the poem "Helping." Student-drawn owl silhouettes would correspond well with *Owl Moon.*

Throughout this book, ideas highlighted with the symbol shown here indicate good bulletin board ideas. Display what your class has fun with! Take advantage of your students' daily efforts by making them double as effective bulletin board displays.

1

September

MOJA MEANS ONE: A SWAHILI COUNTING BOOK
by Muriel Feelings
Illustrated by Tom Feelings
(New York: Dial Books for Young Readers, 1971)
Caldecott Honor Book, 1972

This Swahili counting book is a tribute to the heritage of East Africa. The illustrations for the numbers one through ten depict various facets of East African life such as clothing, musical instruments, a market, animals, natural products, and geographical features. The introduction orients the reader with factual information about eastern Africa. Children will naturally expand their cultural knowledge as they enjoy this book.

Language Arts Teaching Activities
Skill: Parts of a Book

- Use Idea Sheet 1–1 to list factual information from the introduction. Discuss the author's purpose for including this information. What other countries of the world speak languages different from your own? What information would be important to include in an introduction about those countries? Web your ideas.

- What aspects of East African life are depicted in this book? Find examples in the text and illustrations of food, clothing, shelter, occupations, animals, geography, customs, recreation, etc. List them on the map of Africa on Idea Sheet 1–2. Compare them to examples that characterize the geographic region in which you live. Paint a class mural by dividing children into committees and developing the mural step by step. A geography committee paints a general background. Other committees then add details specific to East African life.

- Consider how the accented syllable is indicated in the pronunciation guide: Why is this important to note? What happens when we change accent marks on American words? Example: di′ gest di gest′, min′ ute minute′, pro duce′ pro′ duce. Write an editorial defending the importance of pronouncing a language properly.

Math Teaching Activities
Skill: Number Words

- Look closely at each illustration in the book. How has the artist used the featured number?

- Chart number words from many languages on Idea Sheet 1–3. Begin to use them during math class. Try skip counting using the foreign number words. Form groups of students for problem-solving exercises. Have each group use a different language to answer their problems.
- Create your own counting book. Combine Swahili numbers with everyday things from your life. Add a pronunciation key that would help an East African child read your book.
- Learn to play *mankala* with friends. What kind of strategy tips can you derive? Share your advice with a new learner.

Social Studies Teaching Activities
Skill: Using Maps

- Emphasize the use of map skills. Define *continent* and *country.* List basic facts about each of Africa's countries. (See "Shoulder Tap Research" in the "Classroom Management" section on page 18.)

- Kilimanjaro is the highest mountain in Africa. Plot it on the Idea Sheet 1–4 map. Research other mountain ranges and add them to the map. Compare Africa's mountains with mountain ranges in your area. Design a travel poster featuring one of the mountain ranges.
- The page in the book that depicts number 8 shows the details of an East African market. Use information from this illustration to plan a classroom market. Form student teams to create market stalls for specific occupations. Invite other classes to visit. (**Note:** For other market ideas, see *On Market Street,* page 137.)

- Consider the clothing worn in East Africa. Chart the types of clothes and possible reasons for wearing those styles. For example,

TYPE	REASON
long	greater protection from the sun
loose	easier to feel cool in the heat

Use this chart to discuss criteria you think East Africans use when getting dressed. Which articles of clothing would you enjoy? Why? What modifications might you make to fit your personal criteria? Are there any that would never be useful where you live? Why?

Science Teaching Activities
Skill: Animals

- List the animals native to East Africa on Idea Sheet 1–5. What do students already know about the animals? What would they want to find out? Spend time in the library discovering new animal facts. Stage a panel discussion to describe what the class has learned about East African animals.

- Coffee is a special plant to East Africa. Why? Draw pictures of the growing and harvesting sequence of coffee. Compare different kinds of coffee beans and ground coffee. Plant a coffee bean and chart its growth.
- Experiment with a variety of charcoal drawing techniques such as line drawing on dry paper, brushing the lines with a wet brush, beginning with wet paper, smudging the lines, shading with different types of lines, etc.
- Evaluate the illustrations in the book for use of dark and light. How does the shading affect the mood or focus of the picture? Complete the following sentence about one of the illustrations:

This picture makes me feel ________________________________

because ____.

Name ______________________________

MOJA MEANS ONE

IDEA SHEET 1–1

Directions: List factual information from the introduction of the book on this outline map of Africa.

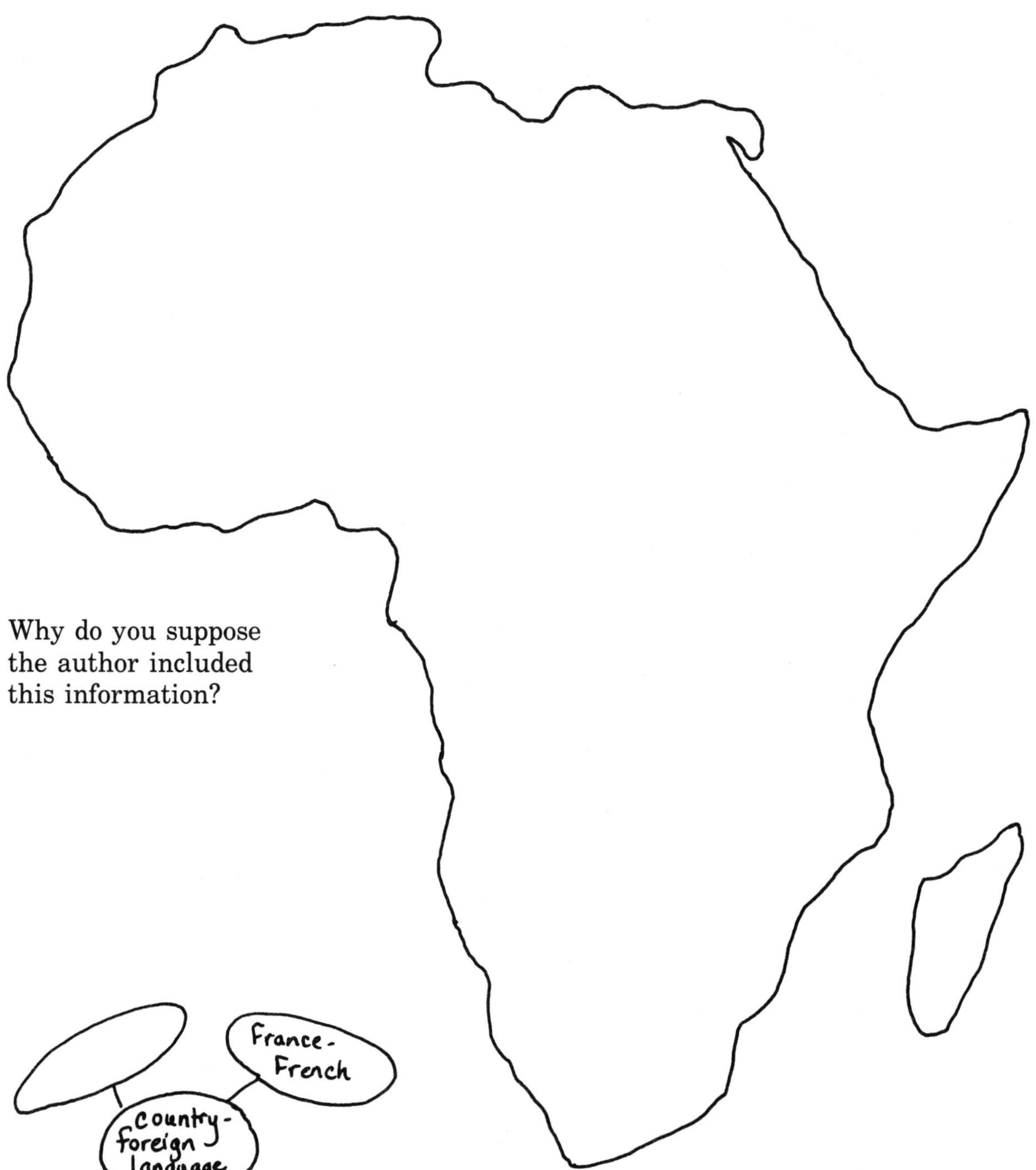

Why do you suppose the author included this information?

Extension: On the back of this sheet, web other countries where different languages are spoken. Choose one to research. What information would you include in an introduction to a counting book of that language?

© 1992 by The Center for Applied Research in Education

Name ______________________

MOJA MEANS ONE

IDEA SHEET 1–2

Directions: What aspects of East African life are depicted in this book? List them on this outline map.

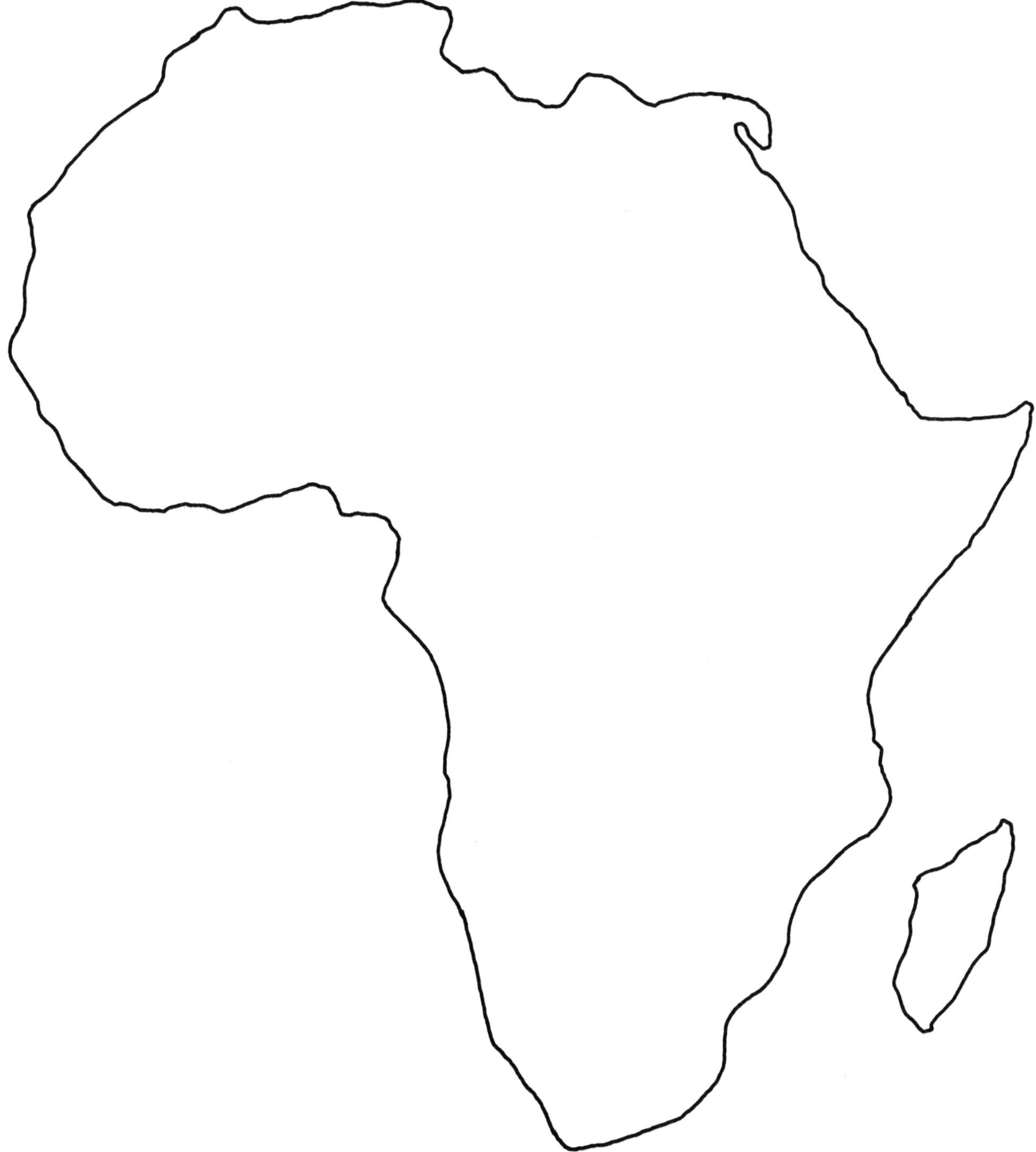

© 1992 by The Center for Applied Research in Education

Name ____________________

MOJA MEANS ONE

IDEA SHEET 1–3

Directions: Choose another language that is spoken in Africa, and list the number words for that language on this outline map of Africa.

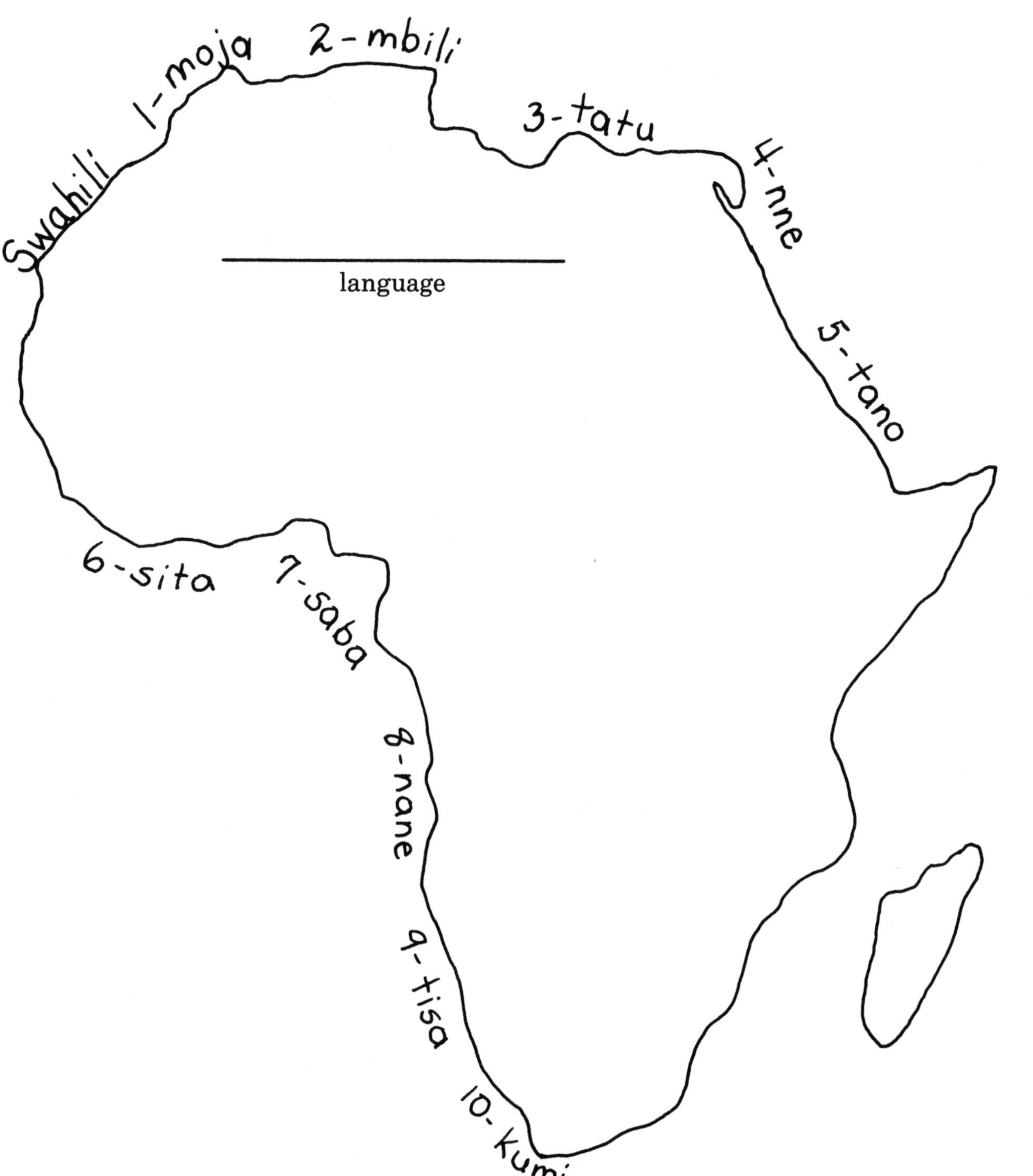

© 1992 by The Center for Applied Research in Education

Name ______________________

MOJA MEANS ONE

IDEA SHEET 1–4

Directions: Plot African mountain ranges on this outline map. List factual information for each one. Research mountain ranges in or near your area. Map them on the back of this sheet with a list of factual information. Compare.

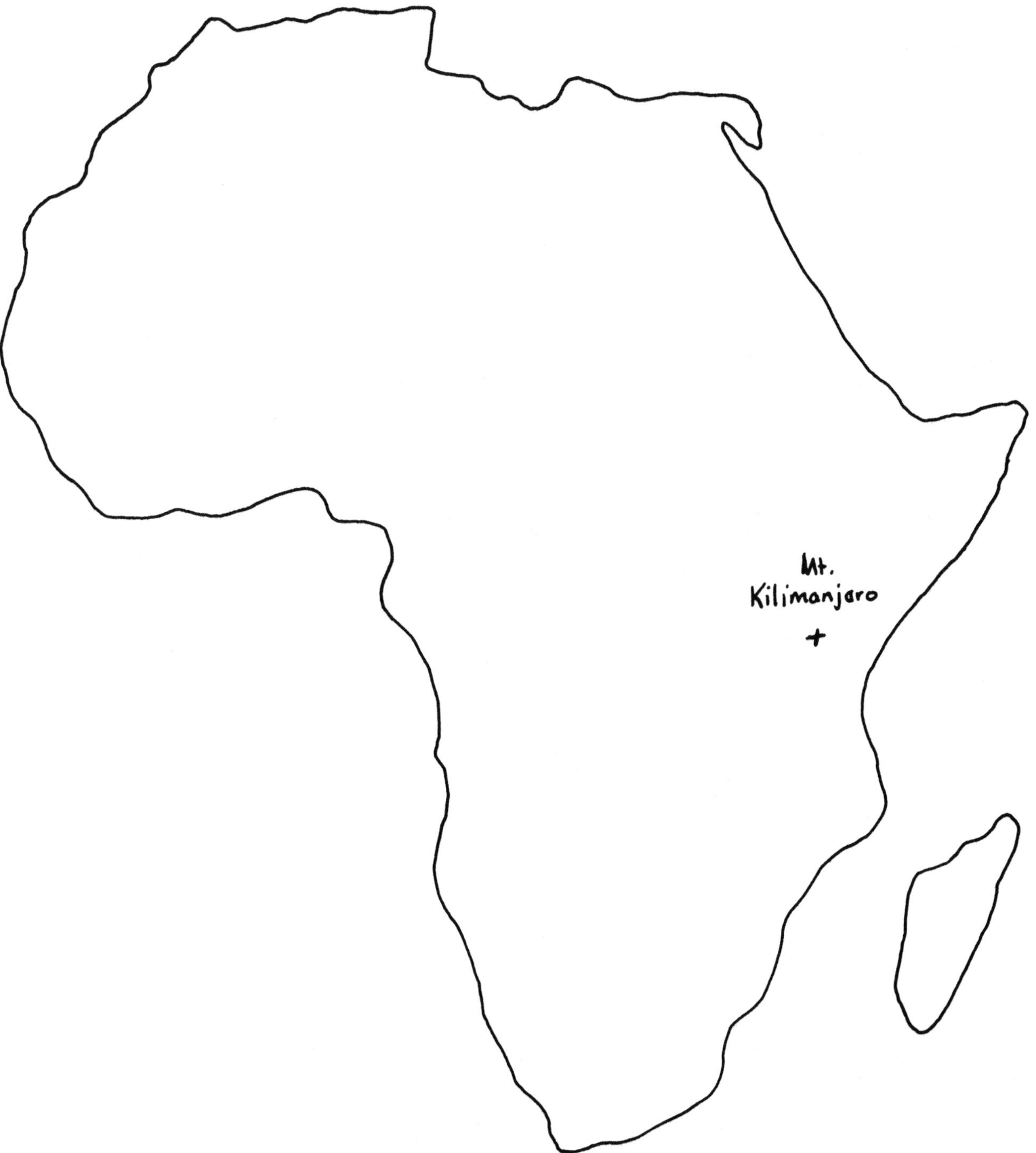

© 1992 by The Center for Applied Research in Education

Name ______________________

MOJA MEANS ONE

IDEA SHEET 1–5

Directions: List animals native to Africa on the outline map.

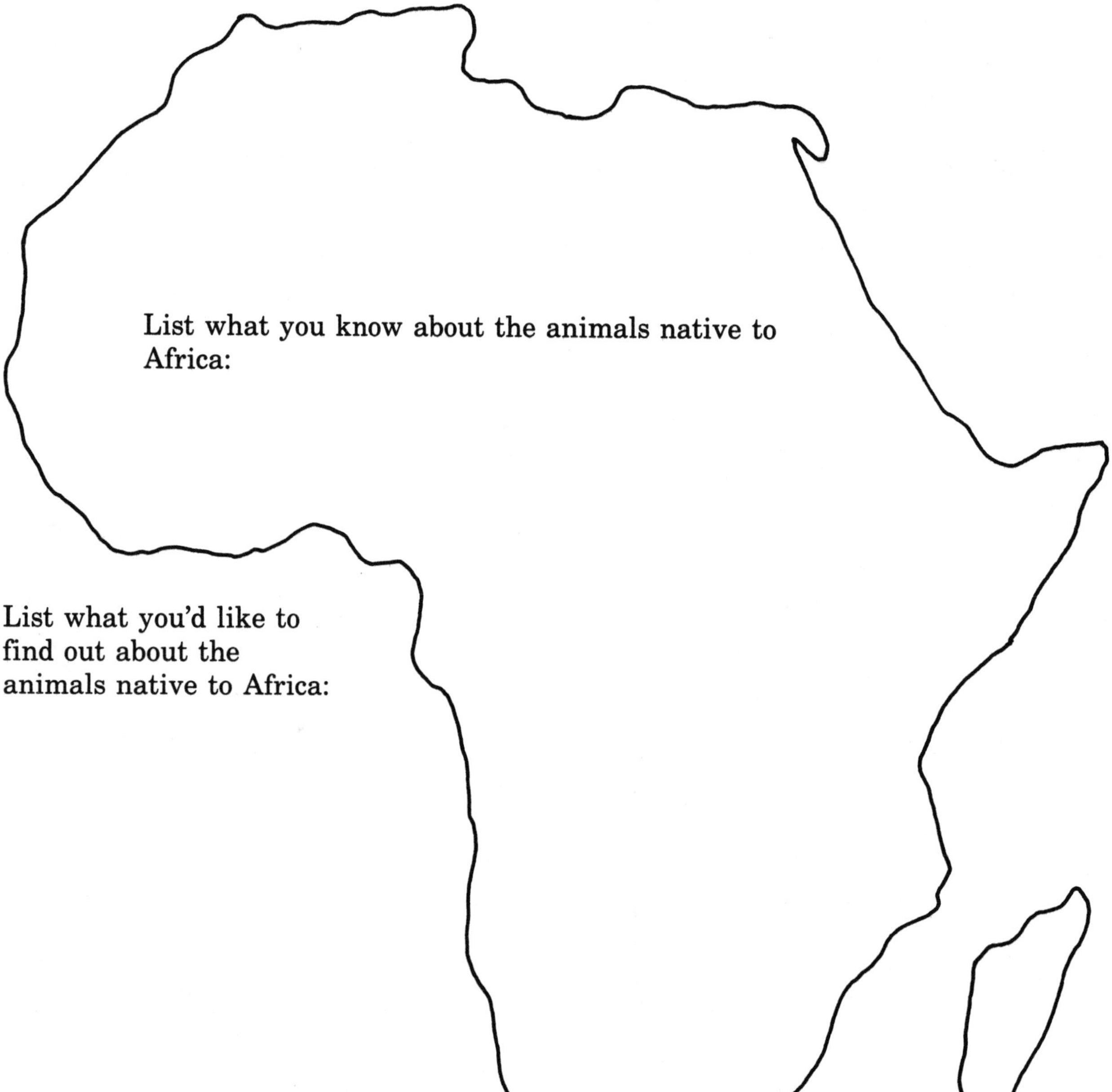

List what you know about the animals native to Africa:

List what you'd like to find out about the animals native to Africa:

Research: List your findings on the back of this sheet.

© 1992 by The Center for Applied Research in Education

Name ______________________

MOJA MEANS ONE

OPEN-ENDED IDEA SHEET

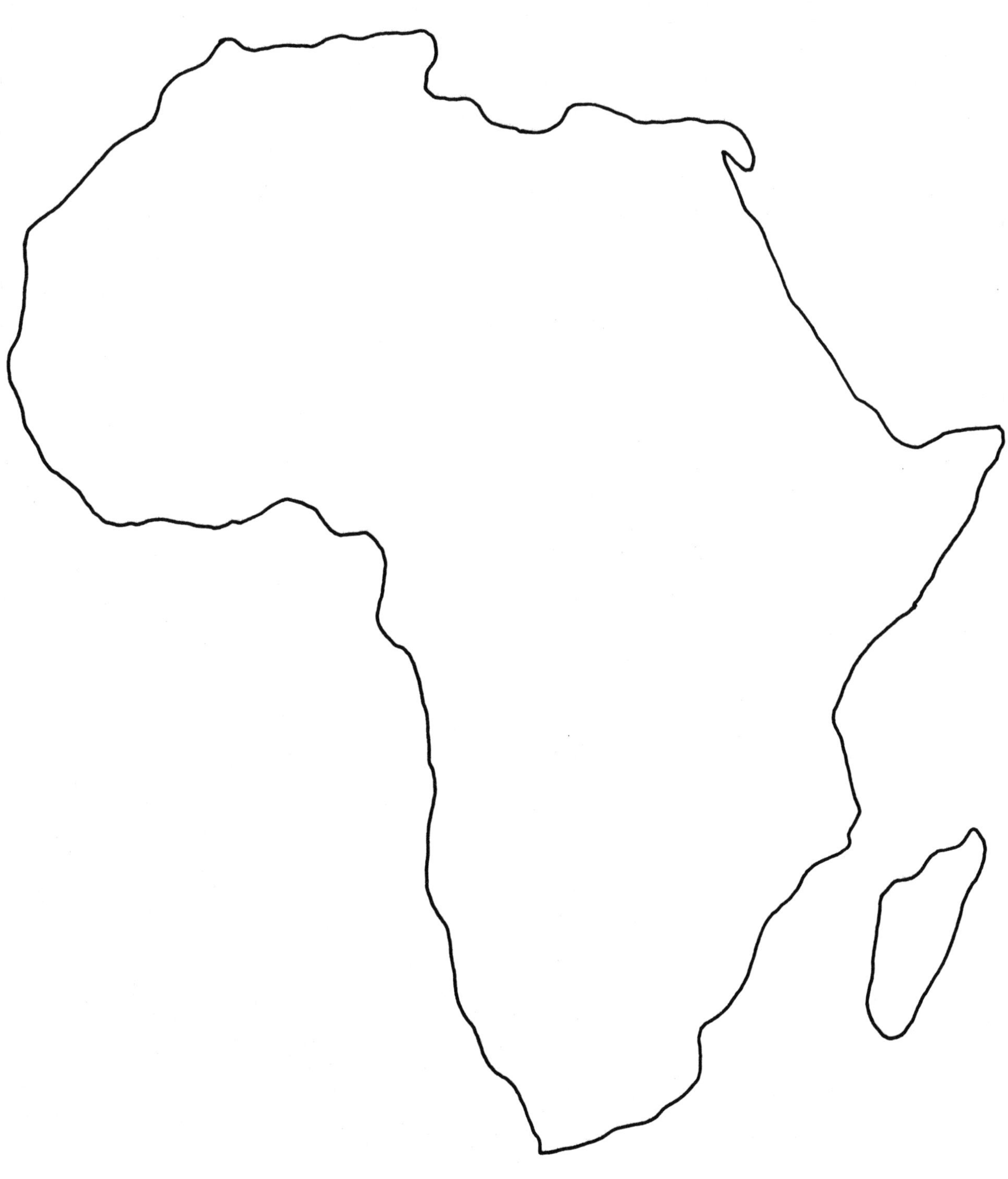

© 1992 by The Center for Applied Research in Education

"Helping"
by Shel Silverstein

Agatha Fry, she made a pie,
And Christopher John helped bake it.
Christopher John, he mowed the lawn,
And Agatha Fry helped rake it.
Zachary Zugg took out the rug,
And Jennifer Joy helped shake it.
And Jennifer Joy, she made a toy,
And Zachary Zugg helped break it.

And some kind of help
Is the kind of help
That helping's all about,
And some kind of help
Is the kind of help
We all can do without.

© 1992 by The Center for Applied Research in Education

MY ILLUSTRATION

"HELPING," FROM *WHERE THE SIDEWALK ENDS*
By Shel Silverstein

(New York: Harper Junior, 1974)

Language Arts Teaching Activities
Skill: Rhythm, Rhyming

- List rhyming words from the poem on Idea Sheet 1–6. Add more rhyming words to the lists. Try substituting some of them into the poem.
- What statements can you make about the words and rhythm of the poem? Analyze these elements and compose sentence strips. For example,

The characters' names all rhyme with their tasks.

- Pantomime the poem and other examples of helpfulness and nonhelpfulness.
- Why do you think Shel Silverstein changed the rhythm and rhyming pattern between the two stanzas? State your opinion and defend it.

Math Teaching Activities
Skill: Measuring

- What kind of measuring is involved in making a pie, mowing the lawn, shaking the rug, and making toys? Chart on Idea Sheet 1–7 the various measurement tools you would use for each.

- Consider the steps of each task. How long would each task take? How much effort would each require? How complicated is each task? Graph your comparisons. For example,

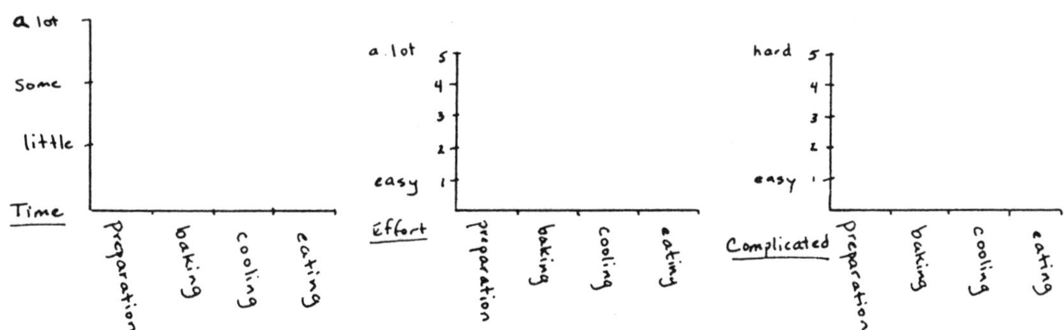

- Write word problems about the four tasks and insert negative elements. Trade with a friend to solve. For example,

> Agatha Fry wanted to make 10 pies. Poor Agatha only had enough ingredients for 3 pies, and her oven didn't work. What are all the things she could do to solve her problems? How many pies could she make?

- Form a judging panel and list criteria for evaluating the word problems. Send the best five to the principal to solve.

Social Studies Teaching Activities
Skill: Jobs

- Consider a variety of jobs and the adage, "Many hands make light work." On Idea Sheet 1–8, draw an example of this from the poem or from your own experience. Cut it into a puzzle to share with a friend.
- Classify jobs that help various people and groups. For example,

CLASSROOM	FAMILY	COMMUNITY	REGION
Wash boards	Take out trash	Clean up picnic sites	Provide public transportation

Which are better done individually? Which benefit from group effort?

- Focus on the beginning of the school year and identify plans for tasks that will help the school, the classroom, the teacher, other students, etc. Make a mobile of your ideas.
- This poem carries a message that some assistance is helpful while other assistance hinders progress. Have students write an editorial of how this applies to personal situations. Collect writings for a class editorial page.

Science Teaching Activities
Skill: Machines

- Make a picture brochure of the various machines used for the four tasks in the poem.

- Compare past methods of completing these tasks with modern methods. Put ideas into a then-and-now book. For example,

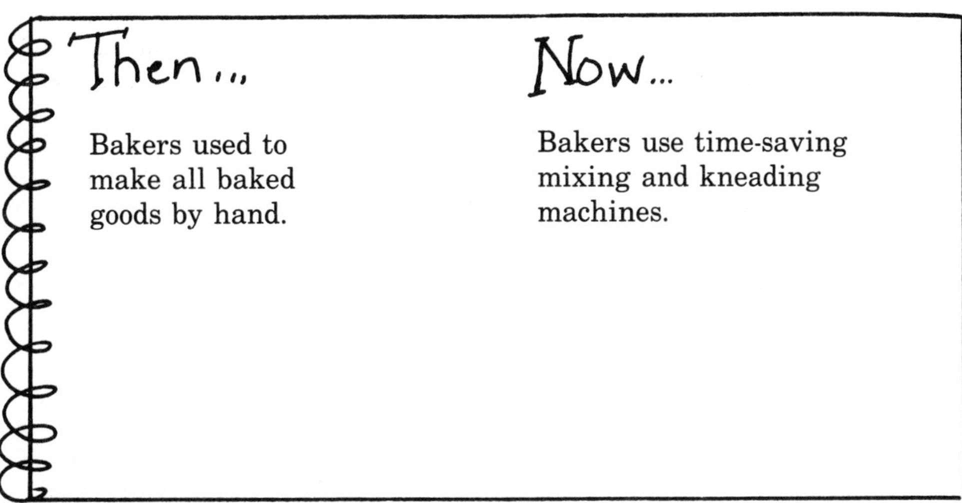

- Invent a machine that would make a school task easier. Show your invention on Idea Sheet 1–9. Share your idea with the class. Choose one person to provide a compliment about your idea and another person to suggest an improvement.

Name ______________________

HELPING

IDEA SHEET 1–6

Directions: List lots of other rhyming words for the poem.

pie
fry

toy

rug

If you get stuck, invent words like Shel Silverstein does!

© 1992 by The Center for Applied Research in Education

Name ______________________

HELPING

IDEA SHEET 1–7

Directions: Chart all the measurement tools that could be needed for each of the tasks in the poem.

© 1992 by The Center for Applied Research in Education

Name ______________________

HELPING

IDEA SHEET 1–8

Directions: How would many hands make light work for each of the poem's tasks? Write your ideas on the appropriate shapes.

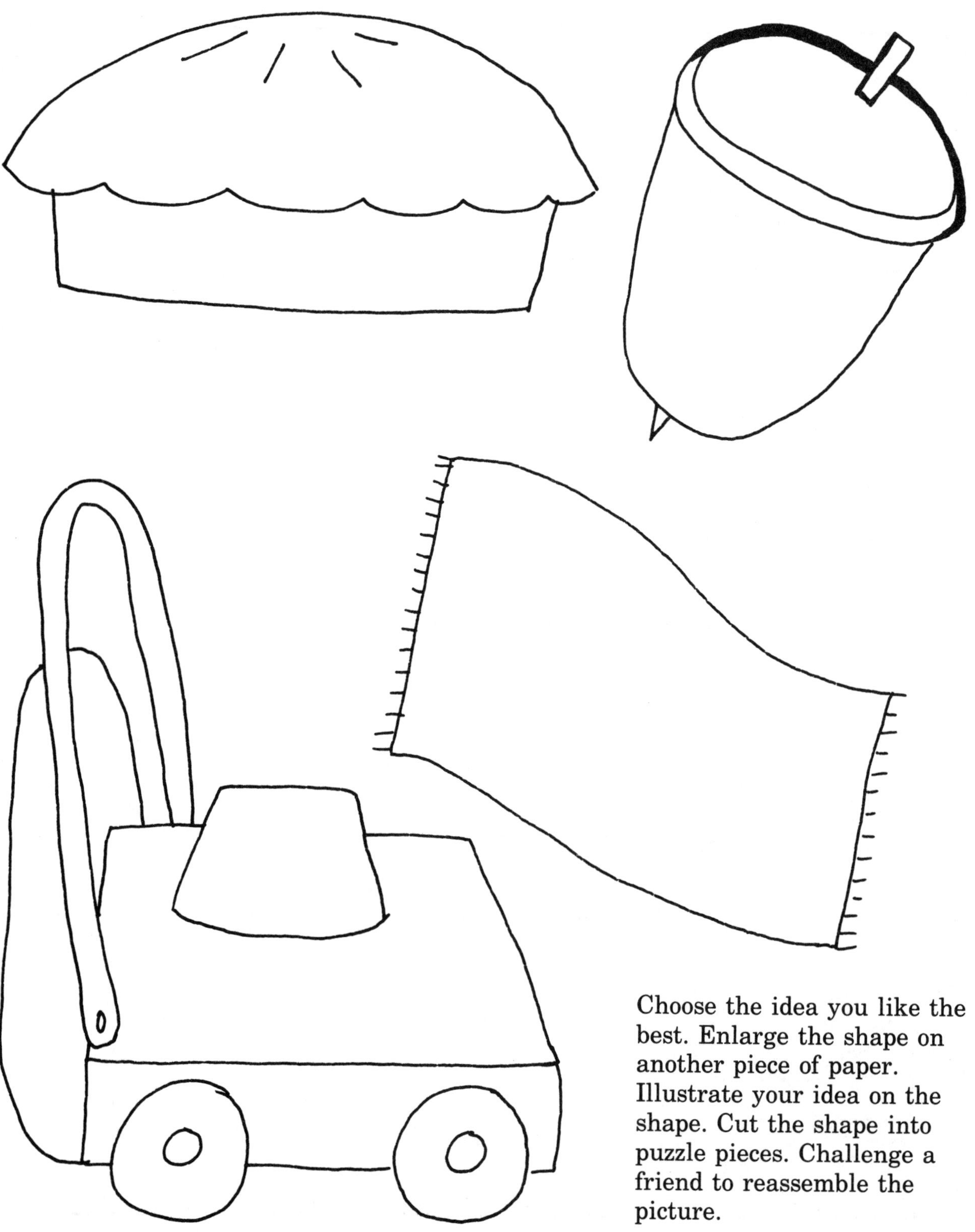

Choose the idea you like the best. Enlarge the shape on another piece of paper. Illustrate your idea on the shape. Cut the shape into puzzle pieces. Challenge a friend to reassemble the picture.

© 1992 by The Center for Applied Research in Education

Name ______________________

HELPING

IDEA SHEET 1–9

Directions: Describe and illustrate a machine that would make a school task easier.

© 1992 by The Center for Applied Research in Education

Share your idea with two friends. Have one friend write a compliment about your idea:

Complimenter's Name ______________________

Have one friend write a suggestion for improvement for you to consider:

Suggester's Name ______________________

HELPING

OPEN-ENDED IDEA SHEET

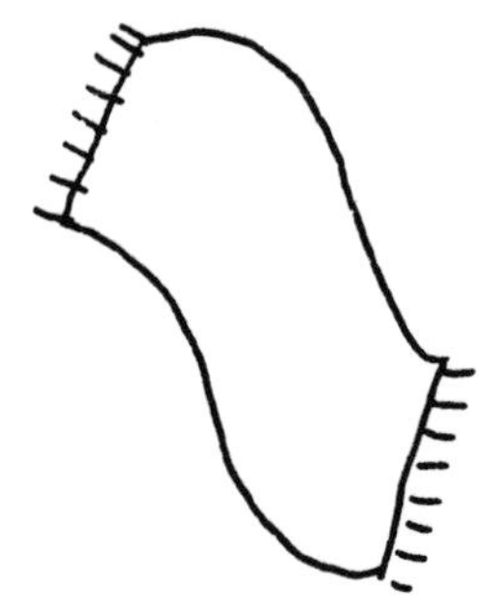

© 1992 by The Center for Applied Research in Education

"I've Been Working on the Railroad"
(Traditional Song)

I've been working on the railroad
All the livelong day.
I've been working on the railroad
Just to pass the time of day.
Don't you hear the whistle blowing?
Rise up so early in the morn.
Don't you hear the captain shouting,
"Dinah, blow your horn"?

Dinah, won't you blow,
Dinah, won't you blow,
Dinah, won't you blow your horn?

Dinah, won't you blow,
Dinah, won't you blow,
Dinah, won't you blow your horn?

Someone's in the kitchen with Dinah;
Someone's in the kitchen I know.
Someone's in the kitchen with Dinah,
Strumming on the old banjo.

Fee-fi, fiddle-e-i-o,
Fee-fi, fiddle-e-i-o o-o-o.
Fee-fi, fiddle-e-i-o,
Strumming on the old banjo.

MY ILLUSTRATION

© 1992 by The Center for Applied Research in Education

"I've Been Working on the Railroad"
Traditional Song

© 1992 by The Center for Applied Research in Education

"I'VE BEEN WORKING ON THE RAILROAD"

(Traditional Song)

This song is actually two songs strung together. "Someone's in the Kitchen with Dinah" is an old minstrel show song, and the work song "I've Been Working on the Railroad" was probably sung by the people who helped lay the track for the coast-to-coast railroad. The two were originally published in 1894 as "Levee Song," perhaps sung by people who worked along river banks.

Language Arts Teaching Activities
Skill: Mood

- Draw a picture of what you visualize from the words and mood of the song.
- Have students compare their drawings. What's the same? What's different? Ask students to verify their thoughts using words from the song.
- Compose a new working song using Idea Sheet 1–10. Substitute words into the song to make it appropriate for returning to a new school year. For example,

    I've been working on this art project
    All the livelong day

- Survey a variety of people–friends, school workers, family, etc. How many know the song? How many are not familiar with it? Propose reasons why this song has lasted through the years.

Math Teaching Activities
Skill: Time

- List phrases from the song that refer to time, such as "all the livelong day." Put these phrases in sentences to describe current school-day activities.

    We enjoy reading books all the livelong day.

- What signals or events indicate the passing of time? The song refers to a whistle blowing. List other examples. Make a catalog of all the ways to keep track of time.

- Consider the phrase "to pass the time of day." Create a class book detailing a variety of ways to accomplish this.
- List examples of when time passes quickly or slowly, and then generalize reasons. Use Idea Sheet 1–11 for independent follow-up.

QUICKLY	REASONS
Having fun at an amusement park	Anticipated fun idea Something you don't often get to do

SLOWLY	REASONS
Waiting in a line for tickets	Nothing to do but stand

Next, make recommendations for how to slow down time or speed up time. For example,

- Slow down: Remark often to your companions how much fun you're having at the amusement park.
- Speed up: Sing favorite songs while standing in line.

Social Studies Teaching Activities
Skill: Cooperative Work

- Draw a sequence of the work involved in building a railroad.
- Analyze how singing makes work easier. What other methods do people use to make work easier? Interview friends and family to list "Making a Load Lighter" strategies.
- Sing this work song with sound effects. For example, add
  - working: sounds of hammering
  - railroad: choochoochoochoo
  - whistle: playground whistle
  - morn: rooster crowing

- Conduct a personal evaluation using Idea Sheet 1–12. What jobs do you do during the day that would be made easier by singing? What jobs would be hindered by singing? List criteria for good times to sing while working and times to avoid singing while working.

Science Teaching Activities
Skill: Sound

- Use Idea Sheet 1–13 to list all the sounds in the song, and cut out construction paper shapes of the machines or instruments that create those sounds.
- Sponsor a Sound Science Fair that features sound. Set up science experiments that deal with sound and invite other classes to visit. For example,
  - What makes a whistle noise?
  - Can you put water glasses in tone scale order?
  - Complete the electrical circuit for a Morse code message center.
- Make your own rhythm instrument. Use it to entertain your parents while they're cooking in the kitchen.
- Invite a doctor to explain how the ear works. What sounds are harmful to the ear? What noise regulations exist in your area? Write an editorial about why sound levels should or should not be monitored and controlled.

Name ______________________

I'VE BEEN WORKING ON THE RAILROAD

IDEA SHEET 1–10

Directions: Change the song into a schoolwork song by writing words related to school activities in the blanks.

I've been working on ______________________

All the livelong day.

I've been working on ______________________

Just to ______________________

____

Don't you hear the ______________________

____

Rise up so early in the morn.

Don't you hear the ______________________

____

"______________________

______________________?"

© 1992 by The Center for Applied Research in Education

Name ______________________________

I'VE BEEN WORKING ON THE RAILROAD

IDEA SHEET 1–11

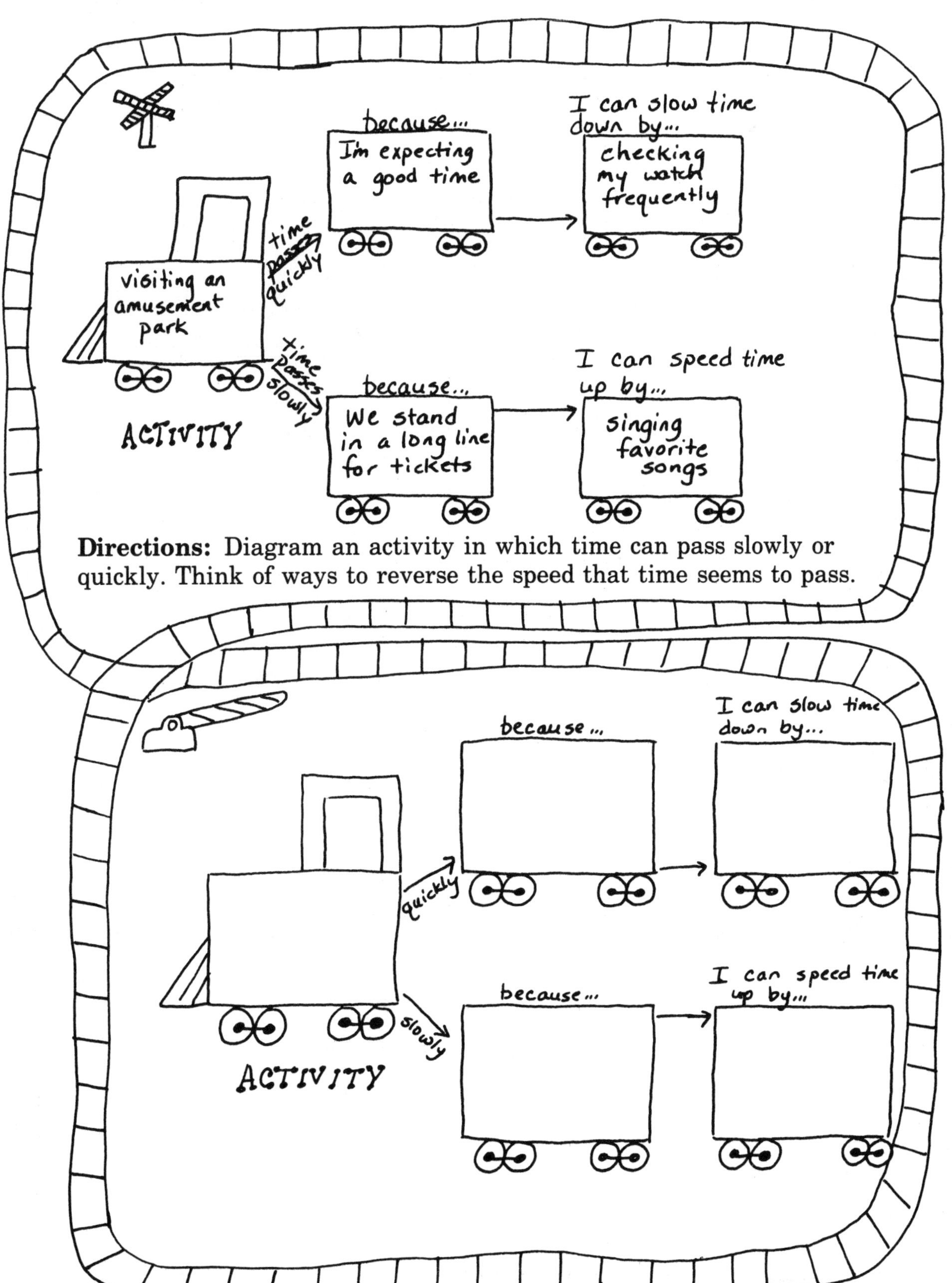

Directions: Diagram an activity in which time can pass slowly or quickly. Think of ways to reverse the speed that time seems to pass.

© 1992 by The Center for Applied Research in Education

Name ______________________

I'VE BEEN WORKING ON THE RAILROAD

IDEA SHEET 1–12

List all the jobs you might need to do in a typical day.	Write how singing would affect the job you do. HELP	HINDER
example: make my bed	*example:* It takes my mind off my work.	It might bother my sister.

Draw some conclusions about singing while working:

© 1992 by The Center for Applied Research in Education

Name ______________________

I'VE BEEN WORKING ON THE RAILROAD

IDEA SHEET 1–13

List all the sounds in the song.	For each sound, list all the machines or other objects that can make that sound.

	List other sounds that would fit this song. For each sound, list all the machines or other objects that can make that sound.

© 1992 by The Center for Applied Research in Education

I'VE BEEN WORKING ON THE RAILROAD

OPEN-ENDED IDEA SHEET

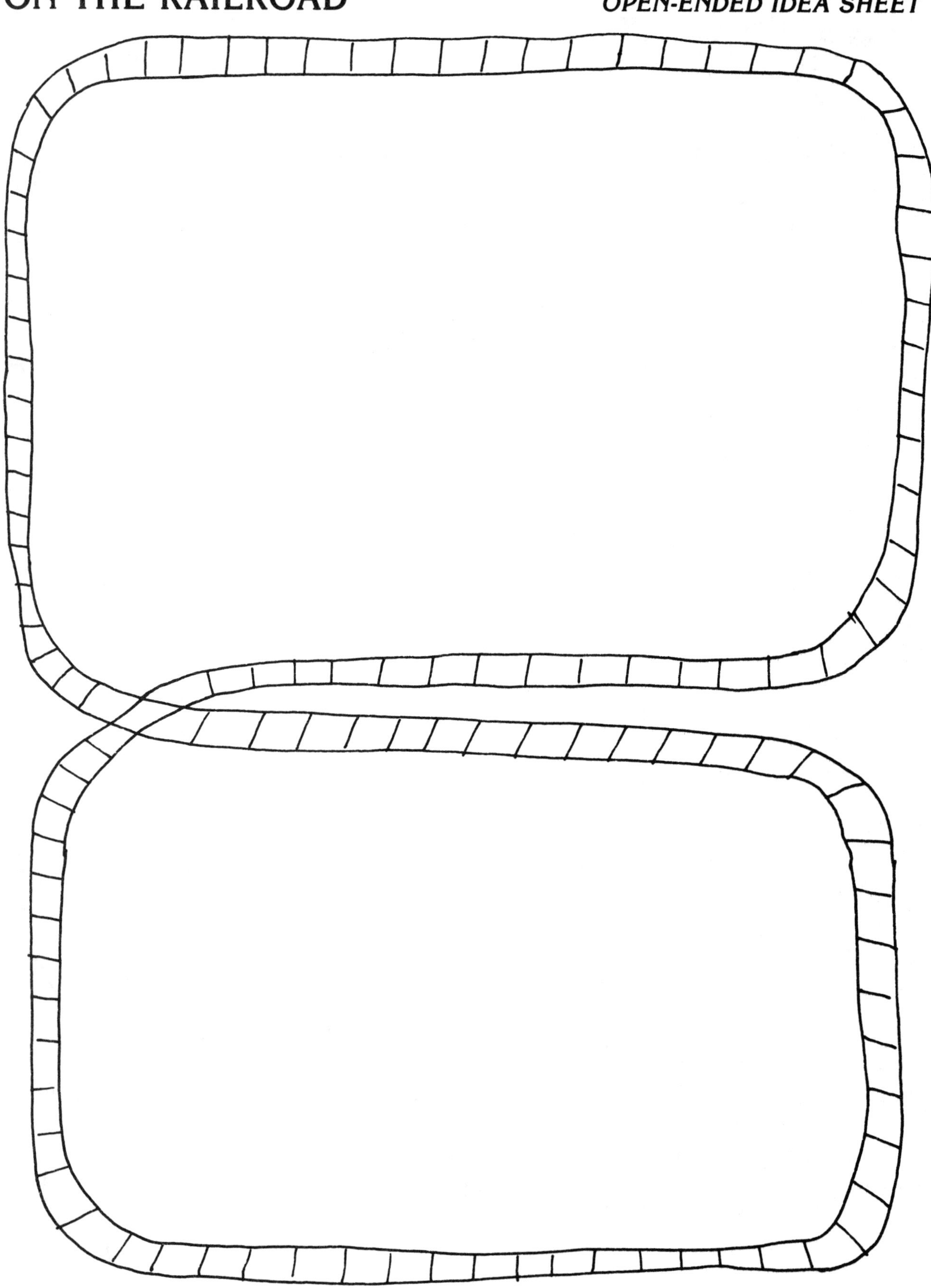

© 1992 by The Center for Applied Research in Education

2

October

THE OX-CART MAN
by Donald Hall
Illustrated by Barbara Cooney
(New York: Viking, 1979)
Caldecott Medal Winner, 1980

Language Arts Teaching Activities
Skill: Story Elements

- Create a timeline of the story. Display it under a mural of the story.

First...	Second...	Third...	

- Enjoy vocabulary study! List vocabulary words on a chart in specific categories, such as farm words, historical words, etc.

Farm Words	Historical Words		
· shear · flax · ox ·	· birch broom · Barlow knife . market		

- Write a diary entry for one day in one character's life using Idea Sheet 2–1. Incorporate vocabulary words in your entry. Share the entry with a friend.
- Describe the mood of the story. What elements of the story support that mood? Conduct a group discussion and consider others' viewpoints.

Math Teaching Activities
Skill: Measurement

- Collect the items (in close approximation) the ox-cart man loaded into his cart at the beginning of the book. Figure out the size dimensions the ox-cart needs to be to accommodate the load.
- Devise a plan for packing the ox-cart by sequencing the items to be packed according to size and weight. Why is weight an important factor?
- Consider the relationship between what was sold and bought. How do the family members use the items?

- Create candles and stitchery products. Utilize library resources for specific directions and designs. Role-play bartering at the market with your items.
- Using Idea Sheet 2–2, evaluate the amount of time each preparation task would take for the spring trip to market. What can you conclude about the May to October activities?

Social Studies Teaching Activities
Skills: Goods/Services Cycles, Historical Perspective

- Diagram the cycle of the story and explain family roles.

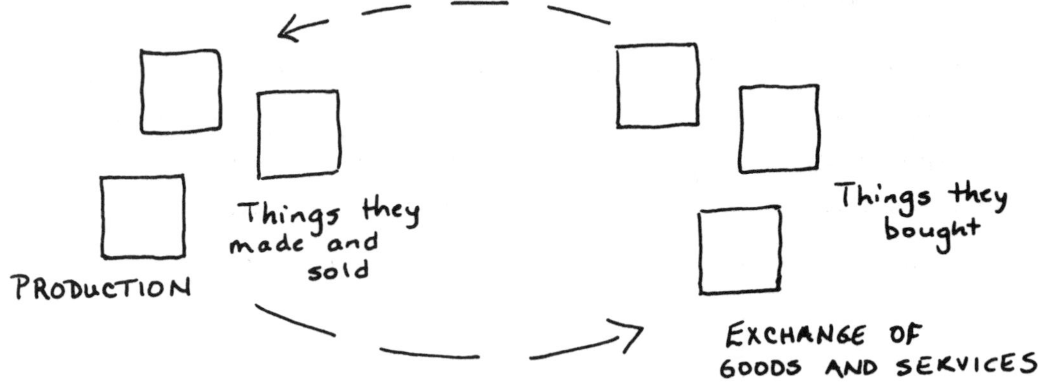

- Compare "then" and "now" aspects of the story. List events and actions from the story and illustrate them. Then illustrate a current idea that corresponds to the event or action. Compile the comparisons in a flip book.

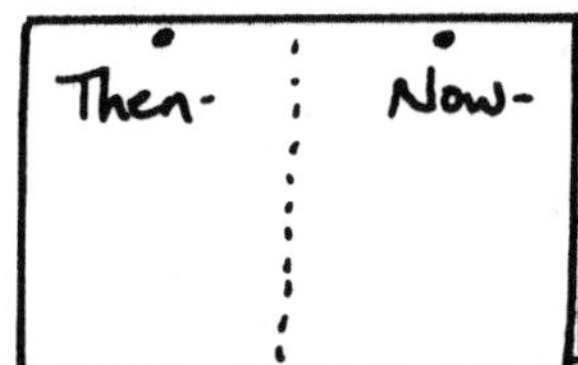

- Look at the pictures in the story and consider what natural disasters might happen to interrupt the cycle of the story. Create cards listing such situations using Idea Sheet 2–3. Take turns role-playing solutions to the disasters.

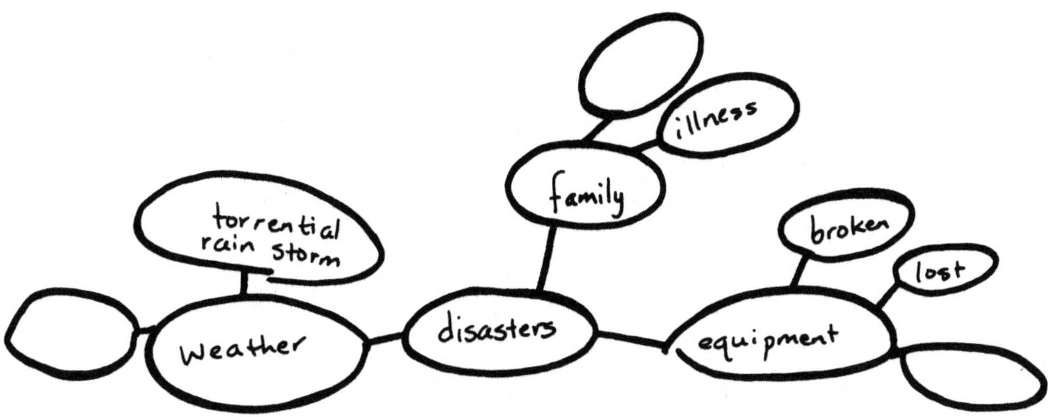

- Give your opinion of the "then" and "now" way of doing things. Which method do you prefer? Why?

Science Teaching Activities
Skill: Productions

- Chart the materials for products discussed in *The Ox-Cart Man.*

material	product	plant or animal
wax	candle	bees (animal)

- Consider each item in the product chart. Which come from plants, and which come from animals? Add a column to the chart to identify plant or animal.
- Consider the natural materials available in the setting of *The Ox-Cart Man.* Invent a new product using those materials (for example, bark–woven mat, feathers–jewelry, etc).
- Compare the economical way the family in *The Ox-Cart Man* used everything in a cyclic fashion with today's recycling efforts. How does the life of the ox-cart family help ecology? In what small, simple ways could we change our lives to live more in tune with ecology? Use Idea Sheet 2–4 to record ideas. For example, the ox-cart man sold the bags in which he carried items; we can reuse our bags at the grocery store.

Name ______________________

THE OX-CART MAN

IDEA SHEET 2–1

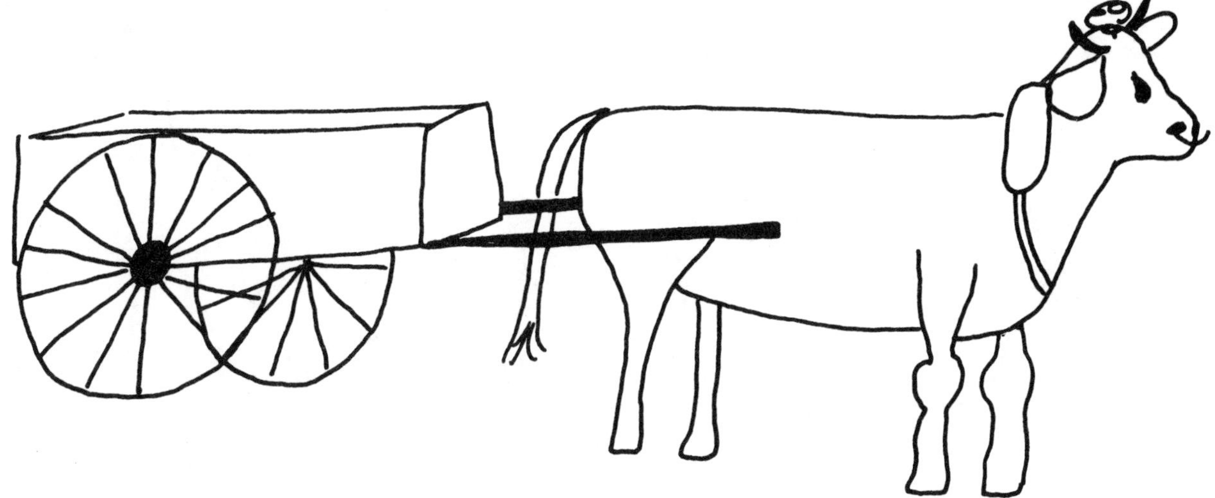

My Diary

Date: ______________________

Directions: Pretend you are one of the characters in *The Ox-Cart Man.* Write a diary entry telling about what you did to help prepare something for the market trip.

© 1992 by The Center for Applied Research in Education

Name ______________________

THE OX-CART MAN

IDEA SHEET 2–2

Directions: List the market items from *The Ox-Cart Man* and the steps necessary to prepare them. Estimate the time needed for preparation. Compare the tasks and time needed. Write conclusions about the tasks and time needed on the back of this sheet.

MARKET ITEM	PREPARATION	TIME NEEDED
Maple sugar	Tap maple trees, boil sap	About 3 weeks

© 1992 by The Center for Applied Research in Education

THE OX-CART MAN

IDEA SHEET 2–3

DISASTER CARD	DISASTER CARD
DISASTER CARD	DISASTER CARD

© 1992 by The Center for Applied Research in Education

Name ______________________

THE OX-CART MAN

IDEA SHEET 2–4

Directions: How does the life of the ox-cart man show respect for the earth? List small, simple ways modern-day people are keeping ecology in mind.

At school: ______________________

At home: ______________________

In our community: ______________________

© 1992 by The Center for Applied Research in Education

Name ______________________________

THE OX-CART MAN

OPEN-ENDED IDEA SHEET

© 1992 by The Center for Applied Research in Education

"This Is Halloween"
by Dorothy Brown Thompson

Goblins on the doorstep,
  Phantoms in the air,
Owls on witches' gateposts,
  Giving stare for stare,
Cats on flying broomsticks
  Bats against the moon,
Stirrings round of fate-cakes,
  With a solemn spoon,
Whirling apple parings,
  Figures draped in sheets,
Dodging, disappearing,
  Up and down the streets,
Jack-o'-lanterns grinning,
  Shadows on a screen,
Shrieks and starts and laughter–
  This is Halloween!

MY ILLUSTRATION

© 1992 by The Center for Applied Research in Education

"THIS IS HALLOWEEN"
by Dorothy Brown Thompson
from The Random House Book of Poetry
(New York: Random House, 1983)

Language Arts Teaching Activities
Skill: Vocabulary

- Draw a vocabulary picture: After enjoying the poem, draw a picture that includes all the images the poem evokes. Label by copying words from the poem onto the picture.
- List categories of words from the poem. Which are nouns, verbs, sound words, etc.? Add your own examples to each list.

Nouns	Verbs	Sound Words	
goblins	giving	shricks	

- Consider the word "fate-cake." Brainstorm all the ingredients that might go into a fate-cake, and all the effects it might have on people. Write your own specialty version of a fate-cake recipe on Idea Sheet 2–5.
- Compliment Dorothy Brown Thompson on the parts of her poem that you enjoyed. Write a letter to her explaining your feelings. Do you have any suggestions for changes or additions to the poem?

Math Teaching Activities
Skills: Sets, Counting, Graphing

- Draw separate sets for the nouns listed in the poem: goblins, owls, etc. Compare the sets using greater than, less than, and equals signs.
- Count and chart the rhythm pattern for each line of the poem. What happens if you interchange some of the lines? What words might be substituted into each line? What words would not work? Why?

- Make the poem a counting poem by adding numbers to each line. For example,

One goblin on the doorstep,
Two phantoms in the air, etc.

- Survey classmates for their favorite character from the poem. Graph the results of the survey on Idea Sheet 2–6 and write evaluative statements using the data. For example, "The class favorite character was __________. The least favorite was __________." **Note:** Try a bar graph, line graph, or picture graph.

Social Studies Teaching Activities
Skill: Neighborhoods

- Make a model of a character from the poem. Create a neighborhood display around the poem.
- Consider each group described in the poem. What neighborhood needs would each have? Chart them on Idea Sheet 2–7.
- Use your thoughts from Idea Sheet 2–7 to map the neighborhood of this poem.
- The last sentence states, "This is Halloween!" Do you agree? Disagree? Why or why not? How might living in America affect our opinions?

Science Teaching Activities
Skills: Sounds, Senses, Changes, Weather

- Collect a variety of materials to create sound effects for the poem. Incorporate loud, soft, high, and low sounds.
- Match phrases of the poem with the five senses.

	eyes	nose	ears	mouth	hand
goblins on the doorstep	✓		✓		✓

- On white construction paper, draw a picture to accompany the poem using a cotton swab dipped in lemon juice. Iron the paper when dry. Why does the construction paper change color? List other liquids that cause changes when used. For example, chocolate syrup turns milk brown, detergent takes dirt out of clothes, etc.

- Generate a list of different types of weather. Describe the perfect weather or worst weather for a Halloween night using Idea Sheet 2–8. Be sure to support your opinion by telling why you include certain weather factors. Could this perfect Halloween night happen in any other season? Why or why not?

Name ______________________

THIS IS HALLOWEEN

IDEA SHEET 2–5

Directions: List ingredients for a fate-cake. Then write the directions for making it. Describe what effect this fate-cake would have once it was consumed.

Ingredients: ______________________

Directions: ______________________

Effect: ______________________

© 1992 by The Center for Applied Research in Education

Name ______________________

THIS IS HALLOWEEN

IDEA SHEET 2–6

15								
14								
13								
12								
11								
10								
9								
8								
7								
6								
5								
4								
3								
2								
1								
	goblins	phantoms	owls	witches	cats	bats	jack-o'-lanterns	other

© 1992 by The Center for Applied Research in Education

Name ______________________

THIS IS HALLOWEEN

IDEA SHEET 2–7

Directions: Consider the groups in the poem. What needs would they have if they lived in a neighborhood? List them and explain your reasoning.

SPOOKS	NEEDS	REASON
Cats	A large open area for take-off space	They ride on flying broomsticks.

© 1992 by The Center for Applied Research in Education

Name ______________________

THIS IS HALLOWEEN

IDEA SHEET 2–8

Directions: Describe and show the perfect weather for Halloween night. Be sure to tell why you chose this type of weather.

rain

lightning

crash
boom
thunder

fog

late sun

clear sky-
full moon

cool
jacket weather

?

© 1992 by The Center for Applied Research in Education

THIS IS HALLOWEEN

OPEN-ENDED IDEA SHEET

© 1992 by The Center for Applied Research in Education

"She'll Be Coming 'Round the Mountain"
(Traditional Song)

She'll be coming 'round the mountain when she comes, (toot toot)
She'll be coming 'round the mountain when she comes, (toot toot)
She'll be coming 'round the mountain,
She'll be coming 'round the mountain,
She'll be coming 'round the mountain when she comes. (toot toot)

She'll be driving six white horses when she comes, (whoa back)
She'll be driving six white horses when she comes, (whoa back)
She'll be driving six white horses,
She'll be driving six white horses,
She'll be driving six white horses when she comes. (whoa back, toot toot)

Oh, we'll all go out to meet her when she comes, (hi babe)
Oh we'll all go out to meet her when she comes, (hi babe)
Oh we'll all go out to meet her,
We'll all go out to meet her,
We'll all go out to meet her when she comes. (hi babe, whoa back, toot toot)

She'll be wearing red pajamas when she comes, (scratch scratch)
She'll be wearing red pajamas when she comes, (scratch scratch)
She'll be wearing red pajamas,
She'll be wearing red pajamas,
She'll be wearing red pajamas when she comes. (scratch scratch, hi babe, whoa back, toot toot)

She will have to sleep with Grandma when she comes, (snore snore)
She will have to sleep with Grandma when she comes, (snore snore)
She will have to sleep with Grandma,
She will have to sleep with Grandma,
She will have to sleep with Grandma when she comes.
(snore snore, scratch scratch, hi babe, whoa back, toot toot!)

MY ILLUSTRATION

© 1992 by The Center for Applied Research in Education

KINSMAN FREE PUBLIC LIBRARY
6420 CHURCH ST.
BOX E
KINSMAN, OHIO 44428

"She'll Be Coming 'Round the Mountain"
Traditional Song

© 1992 by The Center for Applied Research in Education

"SHE'LL BE COMING 'ROUND THE MOUNTAIN"

(Traditional Song)

Language Arts Teaching Activities
Skill: Characters

- Make stand-up figures or finger puppets of all the characters in the song.
- List characteristics of each character on the stand-up figure or puppet.
- Brainstorm a list of all the other things "she" could be, using Idea Sheet 2–9.
- Make a historical timeline of transportation showing how the arrival of "she" in the song could have changed as technology advanced. Predict and support your opinion. Do you think the oral tradition will carry this song into the future? Role-play convincing a music teacher, publisher, or entertainer that the song is or is not still valuable.

Math Teaching Activities
Skill: Sets

- Draw separate sets from the song: horses, townspeople, train cars, etc. Or refer to the following social studies section for a mural idea and identify the set in your class mural. Use Idea Sheet 2–10.
- Compare the different sets using Venn diagrams. Which sets overlap? Which have no connection?
- Create more verses for the song using new sets. Add sound effects as you sing the new verses. For example,

  We'll hang up pretty streamers when she comes,
  (ooo, ooo)

- Which set is most valuable to the song? Take part in a panel debate to explain and defend your opinion.

Social Studies Teaching Activities
Skill: Communities

- Paint a mural of the community represented in the song.
- What other things could be added to the mural? Could they also be added to the song?

- Adapt the song to a different setting using Idea Sheet 2–11. Sing your new verses. For example,

  She'll be coming 'round the corner when she comes,
  (honk, honk)

- Evaluate. How could a song like this encourage community spirit? Why do you think this old song is still a favorite?

Science Teaching Activities
Skill: Chain of Events

- List the chain of events in the song on Idea Sheet 2–12. For example,

  She'll be coming → we'll all go out to meet her

- What other things can cause a chain of events? Illustrate other cause-effect sequences, for example,

  food chain, tornado, change of seasons, etc.

- **Suggestion:** Try cooperative learning strategies with this activity. Have small groups of students illustrate a different chain and share their work with the whole class.

For each chain of events, list (a) the likelihood that it would happen in your vicinity, (b) the direct effect it would have on the classroom, and (c) whether it's natural, caused by people, or both. Then compare your listings. What conclusions can you draw?

- Set a chain-of-events sequence to the tune of "She'll Be Coming 'Round the Mountain." For example,

  In the spring I'll see a bird up in the sky,
  in the sky,
  Well, the bird will build a nest up in a tree,
  in a tree,
  And we'll hear some chirp, chirp, chirps in the tree,
  in the tree,
  The baby birds will fly in a few weeks,
  a few weeks.

- Evaluate the new chain-of-events songs. Brainstorm pertinent criteria; then have students judge them individually. For example, accurately describes a chain of events, is pleasant to hear, etc.

Name ______________________

SHE'LL BE COMING 'ROUND THE MOUNTAIN

IDEA SHEET 2–9

Directions: Make a long list of all the things "she" in the song title could be. Consider people, vehicles, animals . . .

© 1992 by The Center for Applied Research in Education

Choose one item from your list. On the back of this idea sheet, illustrate the song and elaborate upon the "she" you have chosen.

Name ______________________

SHE'LL BE COMING 'ROUND THE MOUNTAIN

IDEA SHEET 2–10

Directions: In the space below, write all the sets of people and objects mentioned in the song. Then draw arrows to show which sets connect with other sets.

Example:

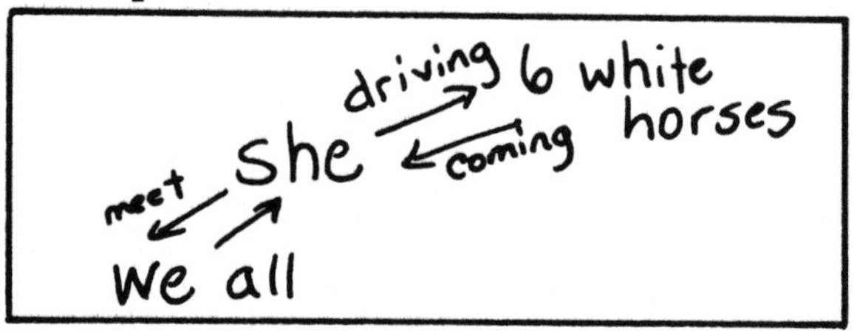

she —driving→ 6 white horses
she ←coming— 6 white horses
she —meet→ we all
we all → she

© 1992 by The Center for Applied Research in Education

Try this strategy with another song or story you know.

Name ____________________

SHE'LL BE COMING 'ROUND THE MOUNTAIN

IDEA SHEET 2–11

Directions: In the space below, make a list of lots of different settings other than mountains.

© 1992 by The Center for Applied Research in Education

Now try rewriting verses of the song to fit a setting you have listed. For example, "She'll be coming 'round the corner when she comes (honk, honk)."

Name ______________________

SHE'LL BE COMING 'ROUND THE MOUNTAIN

IDEA SHEET 2–12

Directions: Diagram the chain of events told in the song by putting one event in each link.

Diagram other chains of events you can think of!

© 1992 by The Center for Applied Research in Education

Name ______________________________

SHE'LL BE COMING 'ROUND THE MOUNTAIN

OPEN-ENDED IDEA SHEET

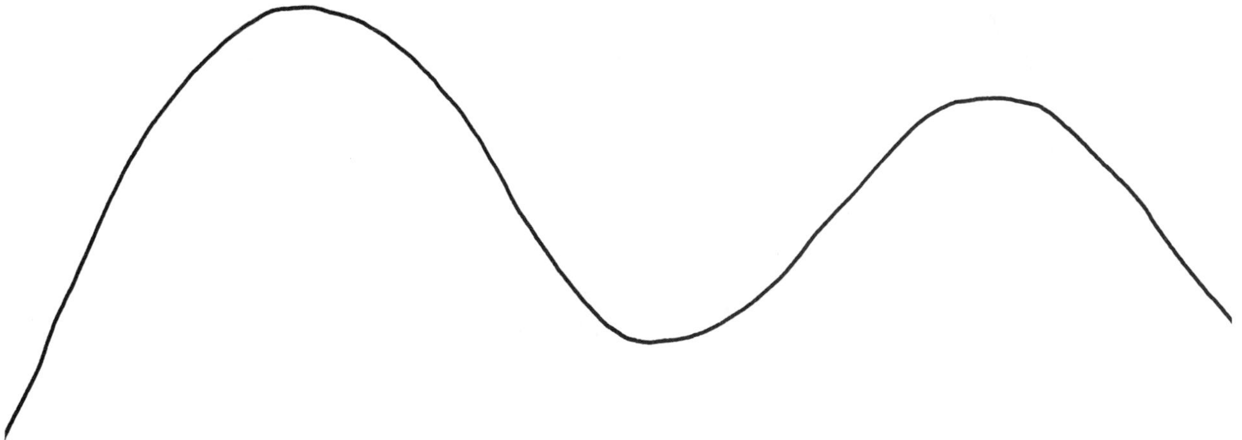

© 1992 by The Center for Applied Research in Education

3

November

ALWAYS ROOM FOR ONE MORE
by Sorche Nic Leodhas
Illustrated by Nonny Hogrogian
(New York: Holt, Rinehart and Winston, 1965)
Caldecott Medal Winner, 1966

Lachie MacLachlan lives in a "wee house in the heather" with his family of twelve. He welcomes every passing traveler to stay through stormy nights. One night, when the house is filled to the seams, it bursts and everyone tumbles out. Undaunted, Lachie MacLachlan and his friends rebuild his house twice the size of the original, and all exclaim that "there's always room for one more." The text of this story comes from an old Scottish song. A glossary defines the Scottish terms. Readers not only expand their vocabulary but enjoy the rhythmic reading of a folk song.

Language Arts Teaching Activities
Skill: Vocabulary

- Have children create Lachie MacLachlan puppets and enjoy a choral reading of the story. Discuss the oral tradition of folklore.
- Enjoy an analytical game using the terms defined in the glossary. Using Idea Sheet 3-1, have children propose definitions for the words using only

context clues. Then compare their definitions to the true meaning given in the glossary. Are their perceptions of the words correct? Why or why not?

- Adapt the song to a holiday when families gather in large groups. Use the tune at the back of the book and add words particular to Thanksgiving, Hannukah, birthday celebrations, etc.
- Why is Lachie MacLachlan's generosity such a good example for his children? his wife? his neighbors? Make a four-sided stabile and describe reasons why Lachie's generosity is important. Contrast the viewpoints of the main character as an individual, a father, a husband, and a neighbor.

Math Teaching Activities
Skill: Measurement

- Illustrate Lachie MacLachlan's home. If it were half the size of the classroom, and most of the visitors were the same height as the average child in your class, what would be the volume of his home? How many visitors would it take for the house to bulge at the seams?
- Make several small houses all exactly the same dimensions but using different materials such as milk cartons, rubber bands, toothpicks, etc.

For each different type of house, what's the point at which there's no room for one more? What withstands a crowd better?

- Use Idea Sheet 3–2 to design your own version of an "Always Room for One More" house. What special features would you include? Make the measurements true to scale.
- Evaluate the ways people stretch their living spaces in today's world. Consider the use of mirrors, closet systems, and furniture that serves more than one purpose. Propose a plan to make part of your bedroom more space efficient.

Social Studies Teaching Activities
Skill: Culture, Occupations, and Geography of Scotland

- Focus on Scotland. Research facts about geography, people, customs, occupations, food, etc. Compile them into a travel brochure.
- Define the various occupations described in the story: tinker, tailor, sailor, gallowglass, fishing lass, peat-cutter, and shepherd laddie. Chart a similar occupation in modern-day society using Idea Sheet 3–3. Draw conclusions: What responsibilities are the same? What's changed?
- Write a script for a conversation guests at Lachie MacLachlan's house might have. Dress appropriately and stage the song found in the back of the book. After the class chants the song, spotlight two characters at a time with a flashlight and eavesdrop on their conversation.
- Encourage students to consider what occupation they would have chosen if they had lived in the days of Lachie MacLachlan. Have them explain the reasons for their choice.

Science Teaching Activities
Skill: Weather

- The weather in this story is stormy. Make a booklet of different types of storms and the effects they have on travelers.
- Use weather information from an almanac or an encyclopedia to compare Scotland's weather with the climate in which you live. Record your findings on Idea Sheet 3–4.
- Use watercolors, chalk, and ink to create a stormy picture.
- Survey people for their attitudes about different kinds of storms. Assess why they choose different activities for different storms. Put the informa-

tion together into a flowchart that shows the different activities corresponding to different opinions. Which line of thinking do you follow? Why? For example,

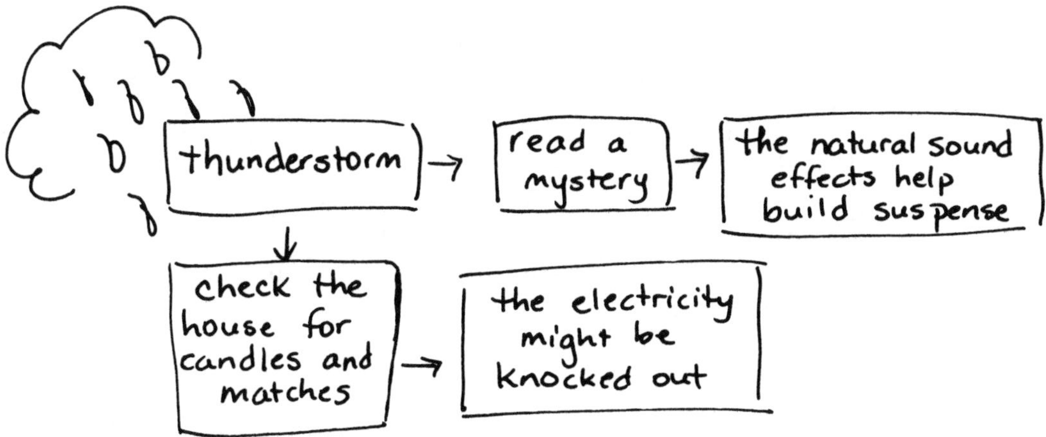

Name ______________________

ALWAYS ROOM FOR ONE MORE

IDEA SHEET 3–1

Directions: Choose some interesting words from the book. List them in the first column of the chart. Make a guess about the definitions and write these in the second column. Then check the glossary. Write the exact definitions in the third column. Compare the definitions in columns two and three.

INTERESTING WORDS	MY DEFINITION (GUESS)	THE GLOSSARY'S DEFINITION
bairns	children	pre-school - children between very, very small and school-age

© 1992 by The Center for Applied Research in Education

Name ___________________________

ALWAYS ROOM FOR ONE MORE

IDEA SHEET 3–2

Directions: Design your own version of Lachie MacLachlan's house. Make the measurement true to scale. For example, 1 square = 5 square feet. Add features such as furniture, fireplace, windows, and so on.

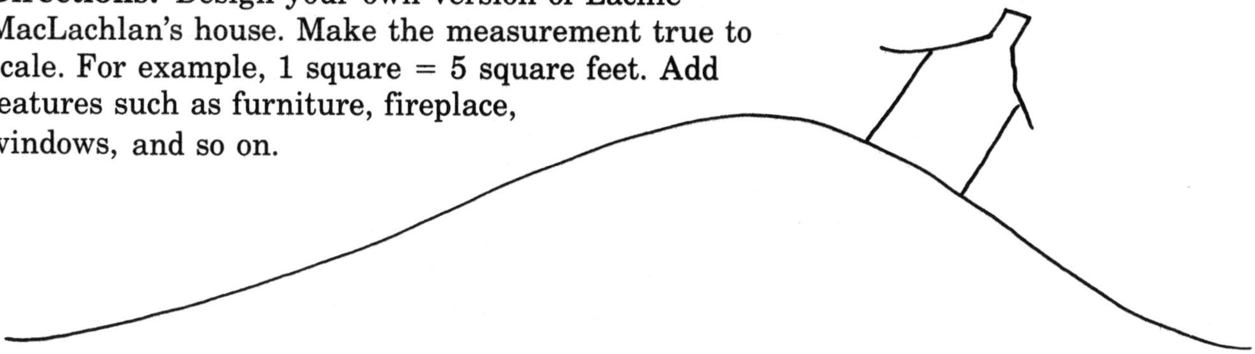

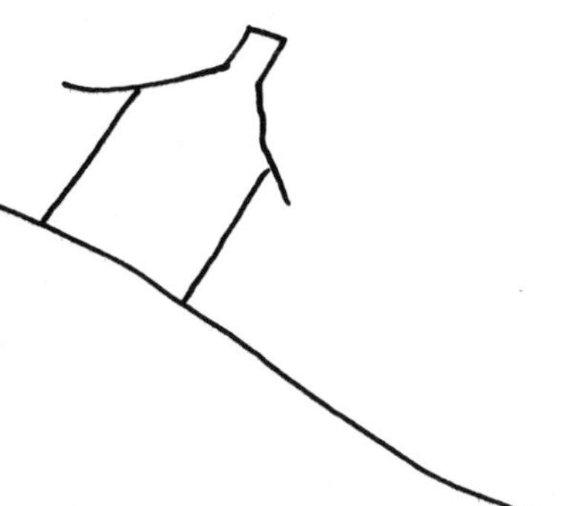

© 1992 by The Center for Applied Research in Education

Name ______________________

ALWAYS ROOM FOR ONE MORE

IDEA SHEET 3–3

Directions: In the first column of the chart, list all the occupations mentioned in the book. Research to find descriptions.

In the second column, list present-day occupations that are similar.

In the third column, draw some conclusions.

OCCUPATIONS AND DESCRIPTIONS	PRESENT-DAY COUNTERPARTS	CONCLUSIONS
tinker - a person who mends pots and pans, makes minor repairs	handyman - a person who can make minor repairs	There is always a need for someone who knows how to fix things.

© 1992 by The Center for Applied Research in Education

Name ______________________

ALWAYS ROOM FOR ONE MORE

IDEA SHEET 3–4

Directions: Check an almanac or encyclopedia for information about the climate and weather conditions in Scotland and in your home region. Record the information on the web below. Add more circles as needed.

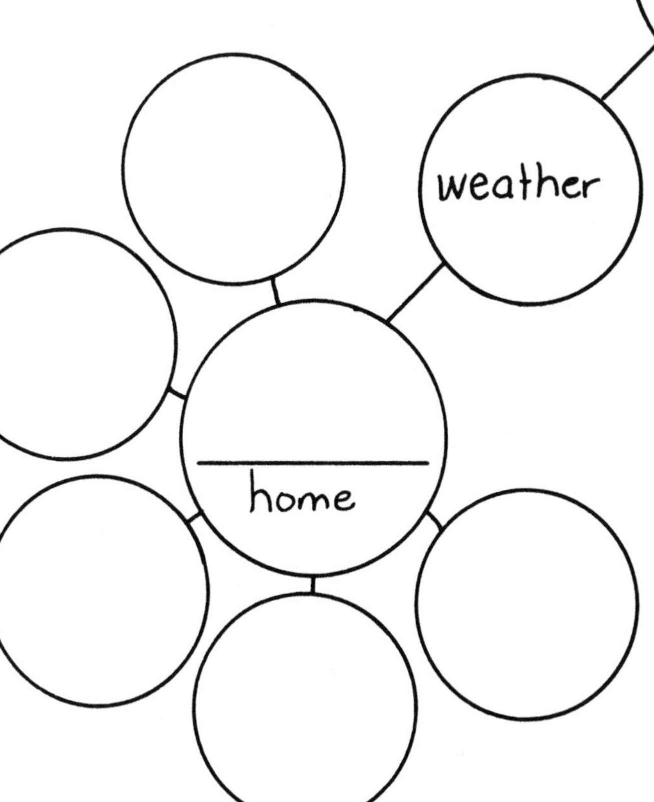

What do you notice about the information you found?

© 1992 by The Center for Applied Research in Education

Name ______________________

ALWAYS ROOM FOR ONE MORE

OPEN-ENDED IDEA SHEET

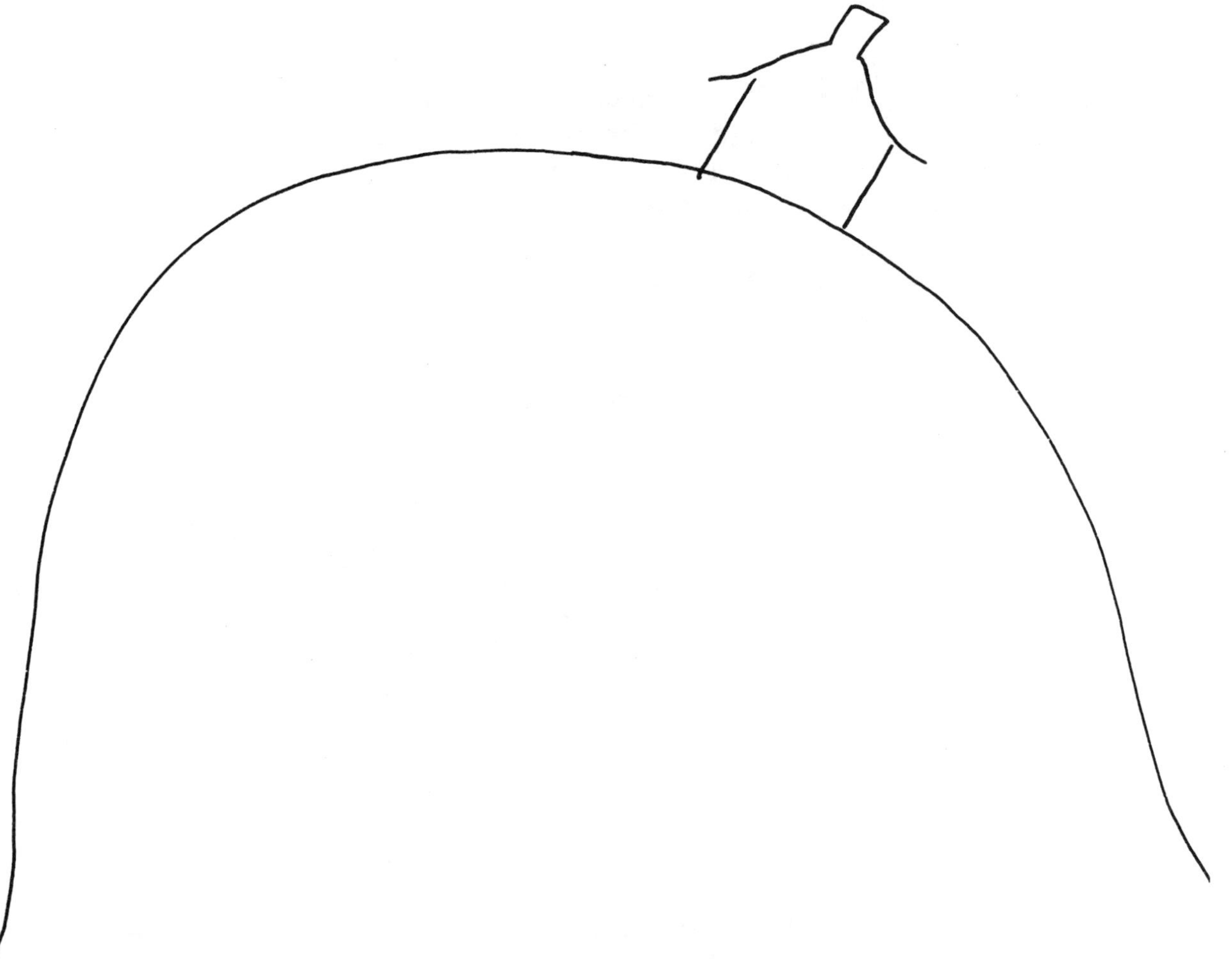

© 1992 by The Center for Applied Research in Education

"The Pinecone Turkey"
by Mabel Maurine Henderson

Once a little pinecone turkey,
  With feathers stiff and hard,
Wished that he could gobble loudly
  Like turkeys in the yard.
They gobbled high, they gobbled low,
  They gobbled with a trill;
And the little pinecone turkey
  Could only keep quite still.

But when he stood on the table
  On last Thanksgiving Day,
And saw a big brown turkey there
  His heart was light and gay.
His heart sang high, his heart sang low,
  His heart sang with a trill;
And the little pinecone turkey
  Was glad he'd kept quite still!

MY ILLUSTRATION

© 1992 by The Center for Applied Research in Education

"THE PINECONE TURKEY," from *Poetry Place Anthology* *by Mabel Maurine Henderson*

(New York: Instructor Books, 1983)

Language Arts Teaching Activities
Skill: Descriptive Vocabulary

- Enjoy choral reading the poem using exaggerated expression.
- Take the viewpoint of the turkey. What details would you add to the poem?
- Consider these words from the poem:

  stiff   hard   high   low   light   gay

  What attributes of real turkeys do they describe? Make a turkey-shaped book that includes these words. Compare the attributes of different kinds of turkeys using Idea Sheet 3–5. Add other pages to your book using descriptive words for wild turkeys, domestic turkeys, and turkeys in drawings or constructed from craft materials.
- In this poem the pinecone turkey is glad he sat still. Make a list of other times when it's good to be still. Discuss your reasoning with a panel of friends.

Math Teaching Activities
Skill: Geometric Shapes

- Use basic geometric shapes and add details to them to create abstract pictures of the pinecone turkey.

- Use Idea Sheet 3–6 to survey friends and discover who has made a pinecone turkey before and who hasn't. Graph your results.

- What other natural objects have the shape of a turkey? (a gourd, an egg, a rock, etc.). As a home project, each student constructs a turkey of natural materials. Display the turkeys at school.
- Collect home-made turkeys for an evaluation activity at school. Have children use the following rating system for the class collection of natural-material turkeys:

Children cut construction paper shapes of a heart, hammer, and dollar bill. Each student places the heart by the turkey he or she likes the most, the hammer by the turkey he or she thinks took the most effort, and the dollar bill by the turkey he or she thinks would cost the most to make. As a class, draw conclusions from the collective placement of the symbols.

Social Studies Teaching Activities
Skill: Traditions

- Describe your Thanksgiving dinner table. Give lots of details. Do your family traditions include turkey decorations? What aspects of Thanksgiving are the same from year to year?
- Begin a new family tradition: Use pinecones to construct something for another holiday!
- Compare the main elements of the pinecone turkey to other traditional holiday symbols using Idea Sheet 3–7. For example, how are a turkey and a jack-o'-lantern alike? (They can both be big and fat!)

- List your favorite family holiday traditions. Why are they so special to you? Write a sentence about each tradition on a corresponding shape. String the shapes together to make a holiday streamer.

Science Teaching Activities
Skill: Pinecones

- Draw pictures showing the story of a pinecone on Idea Sheet 3–8.
- Make a display of different kinds of pinecones and books about pinecones. Compare and contrast different kinds of pinecones in a chart.

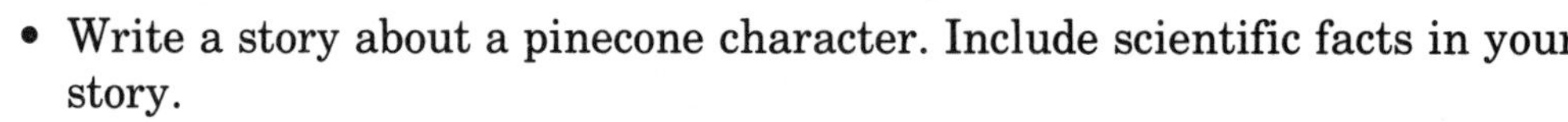

- Write a story about a pinecone character. Include scientific facts in your story.

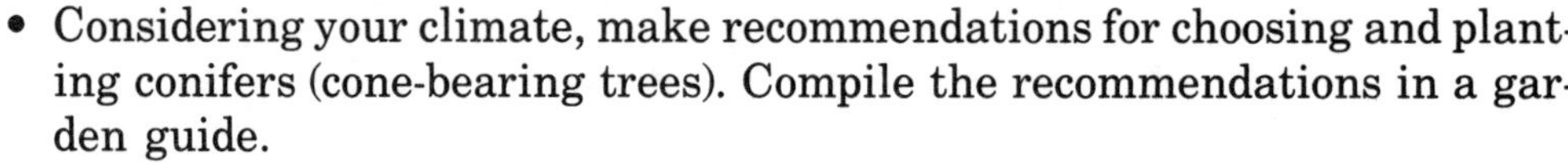

- Considering your climate, make recommendations for choosing and planting conifers (cone-bearing trees). Compile the recommendations in a garden guide.

Name ______________________

PINECONE TURKEY

IDEA SHEET 3–5

Directions: Research to find attributes of different kinds of turkeys. List them on the web.

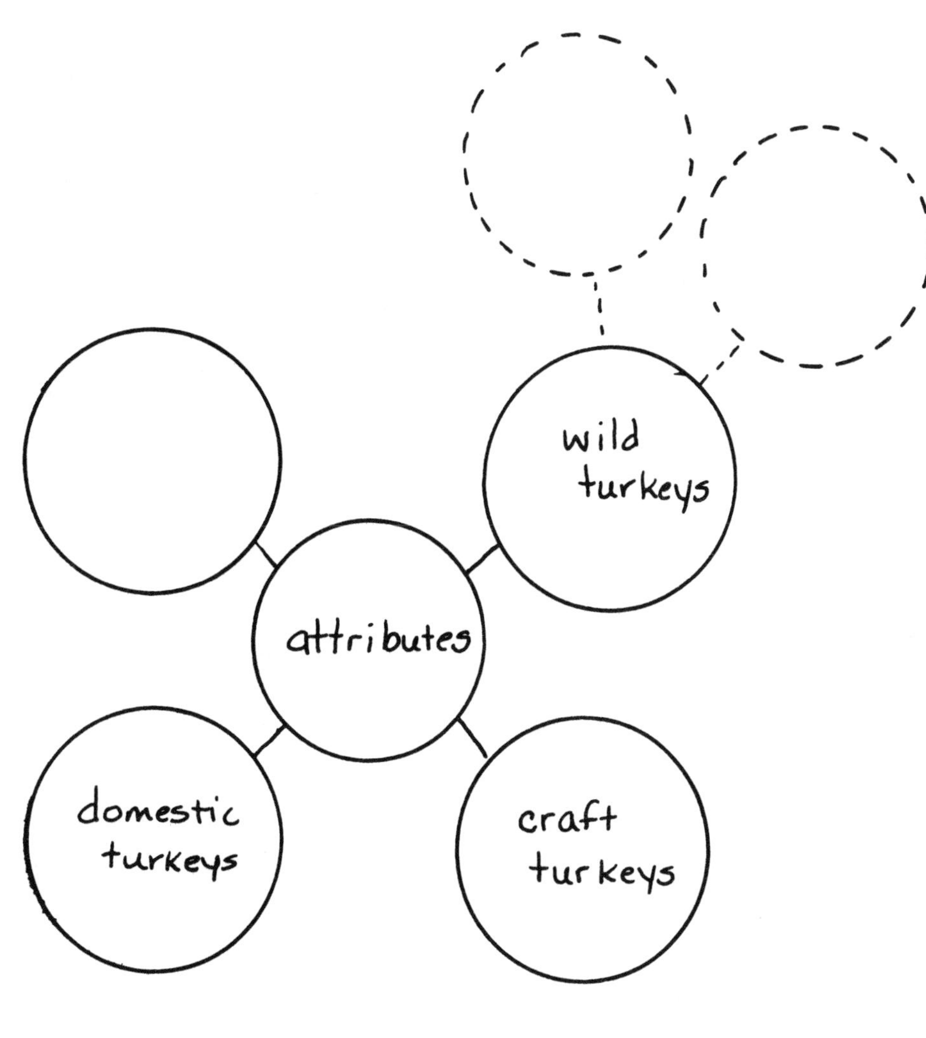

How are *all* turkeys alike and different?

____

____

____

____

© 1992 by The Center for Applied Research in Education

Name ______________________________

PINECONE TURKEY

IDEA SHEET 3–6

Directions: Survey friends to see who has made a craft turkey before. Graph your information.

People Surveyed	never made a craft turkey	pinecone turkey	construction paper turkey	hand-shaped turkey	other	other
12						
11						
10						
9						
8						
7						
6						
5						
4						
3						
2						
1						

© 1992 by The Center for Applied Research in Education

Name ____________________

PINECONE TURKEY

IDEA SHEET 3–7

Directions: On the chart, write words that describe each item.

THE PINECONE TURKEY	THE TABLE	THE BIG BROWN TURKEY

Compare each object from the chart headings to a symbol from another holiday. For example,

A pinecone turkey is like a jack-o'-lantern because they both have faces.

A pinecone turkey is like a ____________________ because they both ____________________.

A table is like a ____________________ because they both ____________________.

A big brown turkey is like a ____________________ because they both ____________________.

© 1992 by The Center for Applied Research in Education

Name ______________________

PINECONE TURKEY

IDEA SHEET 3–8

Directions: Illustrate the story of a pinecone. Add lots of details to show all the possibilities.

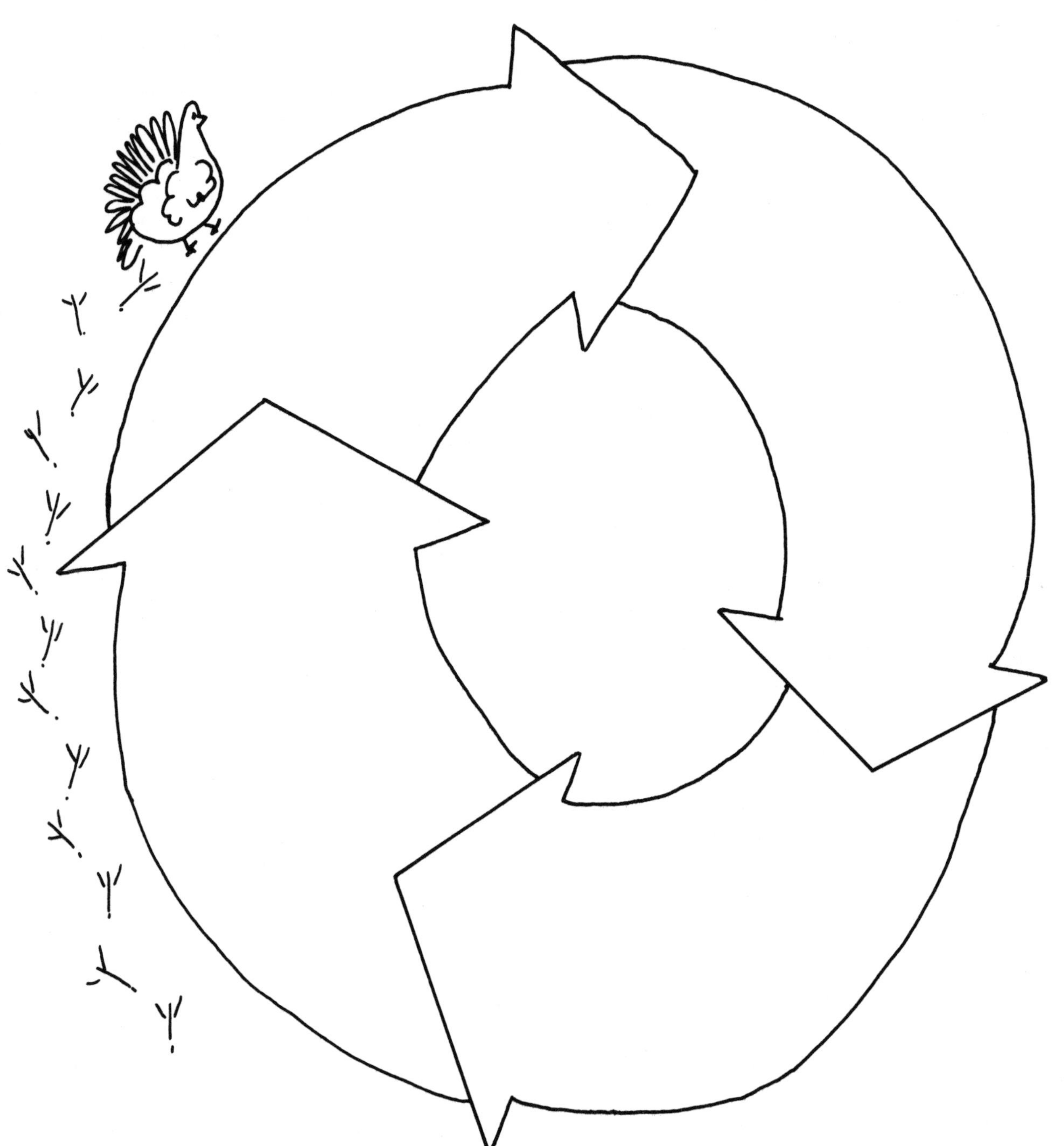

© 1992 by The Center for Applied Research in Education

PINECONE TURKEY

OPEN-ENDED IDEA SHEET

© 1992 by The Center for Applied Research in Education

"Polly Wolly Doodle"
(Traditional Song)

Oh, I went down South for to see my gal,
Sing polly-wolly-doodle all the day,
My Sally is a spunky gal,
Sing polly-wolly-doodle all the day.

Fare thee well,
Fare thee well,
Fare thee well, my fairy fay,
For I'm going to Louisiana,
For to see my Suzyanna,
Sing polly-wolly-doodle all the day.

Oh, a grasshopper sittin' on a railroad track,
Sing polly-wolly-doodle all the day,
A-pickin' his teeth with a carpet tack,
Sing polly-wolly-doodle all the day.

Chorus

Oh, I went to bed, but it wasn't no use,
Sing polly-wolly-doodle all the day,
My feet stuck out like a chicken roost,
Sing polly-wolly-doodle all the day.

Chorus

MY ILLUSTRATION

© 1992 by The Center for Applied Research in Education

"Polly Wolly Doodle"
Traditional Song

© 1992 by The Center for Applied Research in Education

"POLLY WOLLY DOODLE"

(Traditional Song)

Language Arts Teaching Activities
Skill: Vocabulary Mood

- Define the terms *spunky gal, carpet tack, chicken roost,* and *fairy fay* on music notes big enough to display on a bulletin board. Have children illustrate themselves getting ready for a trip "down South" to add to the display.
- Consider the mood of the song using Idea Sheet 3–9. Which words make the song bouncy? Which are nonsense? Which could have a serious meaning?
- "Polly-wolly-doodle" is a funny phrase consisting of six syllables. What other phrases can you think of to fit into the song?
- Survey friends and family. Who likes the song? Why? Who does not like the song? Why?

Math Teaching Activities
Skills: Map Distances, Rhythms

- Use Idea Sheet 3–10 for a distance study. Calculate the distance from your location to Louisiana and other southern states. Which is the closest? farthest?
- Count the syllables in the song and analyze the rhythm pattern.
- Enjoy a class rhythm band rendition of the song. Include a variety of sounds: blocks, spoons, bells, etc. Try the song at different tempos.

- In your opinion, which southern location would be best to target for a pretend trip? Why?

Social Studies Teaching Activities
Skill: The South

- Identify "down south" on a map.
- Research the natural products, resources, and tourist attractions of a southern state. Organize the information into a travel brochure.

- Substitute information from the travel brochures into the song. Intersperse the new verses with the traditional verses while singing. For example,

♫ Oh, I went down south to see Disney World
Sing polly-wolly-doodle all the day,
It was fun to watch the flags unfurled...

- Using Idea Sheet 3–11, have students use the travel information to prioritize places to see. What criteria did they use for their decisions?

Science Teaching Activities
Skill: Natural Features of the South

- Take the viewpoint of a scientist. What plants, animals, and geological features would one see while traveling in the South? Which of the features are native only to the South? Why? Use Idea Sheet 3–12 to record your ideas.

- *The Guinness Book of World Records* lists a variety of natural records. What records might a scientist discover while touring the South? (for example, the longest alligator, the largest peach, etc.)
- Plan a natural science museum for the South. What should be included? How should the building be arranged? Where should it be located? Write a proposal, draw a floorplan, or make a model. Have students explain their reasoning.

Name ______________________________

POLLY WOLLY DOODLE

IDEA SHEET 3–9

Directions: Consider the mood of the song. List words from the song that are bouncy, nonsense, serious, and ____________.
(your idea)

bouncy words

nonsense words

serious words

? words

© 1992 by The Center for Applied Research in Education

Name ____________________

POLLY WOLLY DOODLE

IDEA SHEET 3–10

Directions: Calculate the distance from your hometown to Louisiana and five other southern locations of your choice.

? ____________ to Louisiana = _____ miles

____________ to ____________ = _____ miles

____________ to ____________ = _____ miles

____________ to ____________ = _____ miles

____________ to ____________ = _____ miles

____________ to ____________ = _____ miles

Which is closest?
Which is farthest?
What other comparisons can you make?

© 1992 by The Center for Applied Research in Education

Name ______________________

POLLY WOLLY DOODLE

IDEA SHEET 3–11

Directions: Use travel brochures to learn more about places to visit in the South. Prioritize places to visit. Explain the criteria used to set your priorities.

PLACES TO VISIT	MY PRIORITIZED LIST OF WHERE I WOULD LIKE TO TRAVEL

THE REASONS FOR MY CHOICES INCLUDE

© 1992 by The Center for Applied Research in Education

Name ______________________________

POLLY WOLLY DOODLE

IDEA SHEET 3–12

Directions: Use travel brochures and other resources to list plants, animals, and geographic features a person would see when traveling in the South.

© 1992 by The Center for Applied Research in Education

♫ PLANTS

♫ ANIMALS

♫ GEOGRAPHIC FEATURES

POLLY WOLLY DOODLE

OPEN-ENDED IDEA SHEET

© 1992 by The Center for Applied Research in Education

4

December

ON MARKET STREET
by Arnold Lobel
Illustrated by Anita Lobel
(New York: Scholastic Books, 1981)
Caldecott Honor Book, 1982

This alphabet book was inspired by Anita Lobel's 1977 Children's Book Week poster. Each letter page shows an elaborate and whimsical Market Street vendor. Children delight in viewing such things as a lady covered with lollipops for L, a prince regaled with playing cards for P, and a vendor garbed in vegetables for V. The wonders and beauty of Market Street are tenderly balanced by the selflessness of the little boy who shops there.

Language Arts Teaching Activities
Skills: Descriptive Vocabulary, Illustrations

- Add words for each item on Market Street. Chant the expanded market list as a class. For example,

apples, artichokes, anise, books, ———, ———, etc.

- Contrast the introductory pictures with the alphabet pictures. How are they alike and different? What do you suppose the illustrator was considering when composing the pictures?

- Create a new Market Street vendor with lots of details using Idea Sheet 4–1. Write an alliterative sentence of what the market person would be saying. For example,

  I have absolutely the most aromatic apples!

- *On Market Street* was inspired by a Children's Book Week poster. What posters have you seen that would make good books? Why?

Math Teaching Activities
Skills: Money, Symmetry

- Use catalogs and advertisements to assign monetary values for each picture in *On Market Street.* If you were shopping, what combinations could you purchase if you had $1, $5, $10? What would your bill total?
- Classify each Market Street vendor as symmetrical or nonsymmetrical. Draw lines or labels to prove your decisions.
- Compose word problems for each Market Street character. Leave a missing detail so readers have to use the illustration to answer the problem.
- Use Idea Sheet 4–2 to judge which Market Street character would be most successful. Why? Define the criteria you use for success: monetary value? item value? happiness value? Defend your opinion.

Social Studies Teaching Activities
Skills: Map Skills

- Draw a map of the marketplace portrayed in this book.
- Compare this marketplace to a shopping mall. Chart the similarities and differences.
- What categories of goods are represented in the market? What additional categories would people need? animals need?
- Consider the boy who is telling the story. What personal qualities can you infer about him? Compare yourself to him using Idea Sheet 4–3. Or show his characteristics on personality scales. For example,

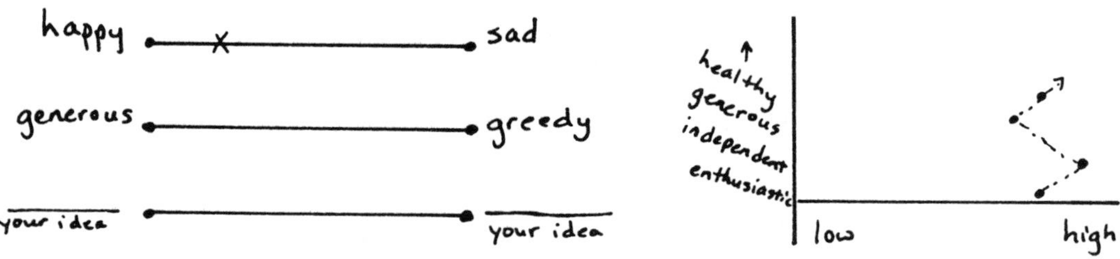

Science Teaching Activities
Skills: Classification, Machines, Weather

- What items on Market Street are nutritious? functional? frivolous? living? nonliving? gas? solid? liquid? What other categories can you think of?
- Have students compare their classifications. (Use the think-pair-share strategy in the Classroom Management section on page 15.)

- Invent a machine using items from each Market Street vendor.
- How would weather affect this Market Street? What do you think the market people do on sunny days? cloudy days? rainy days? What criteria would market people use each morning when preparing for the day? Use Idea Sheet 4–4 to record your ideas.

Name ______________________

ON MARKET STREET

IDEA SHEET 4–1

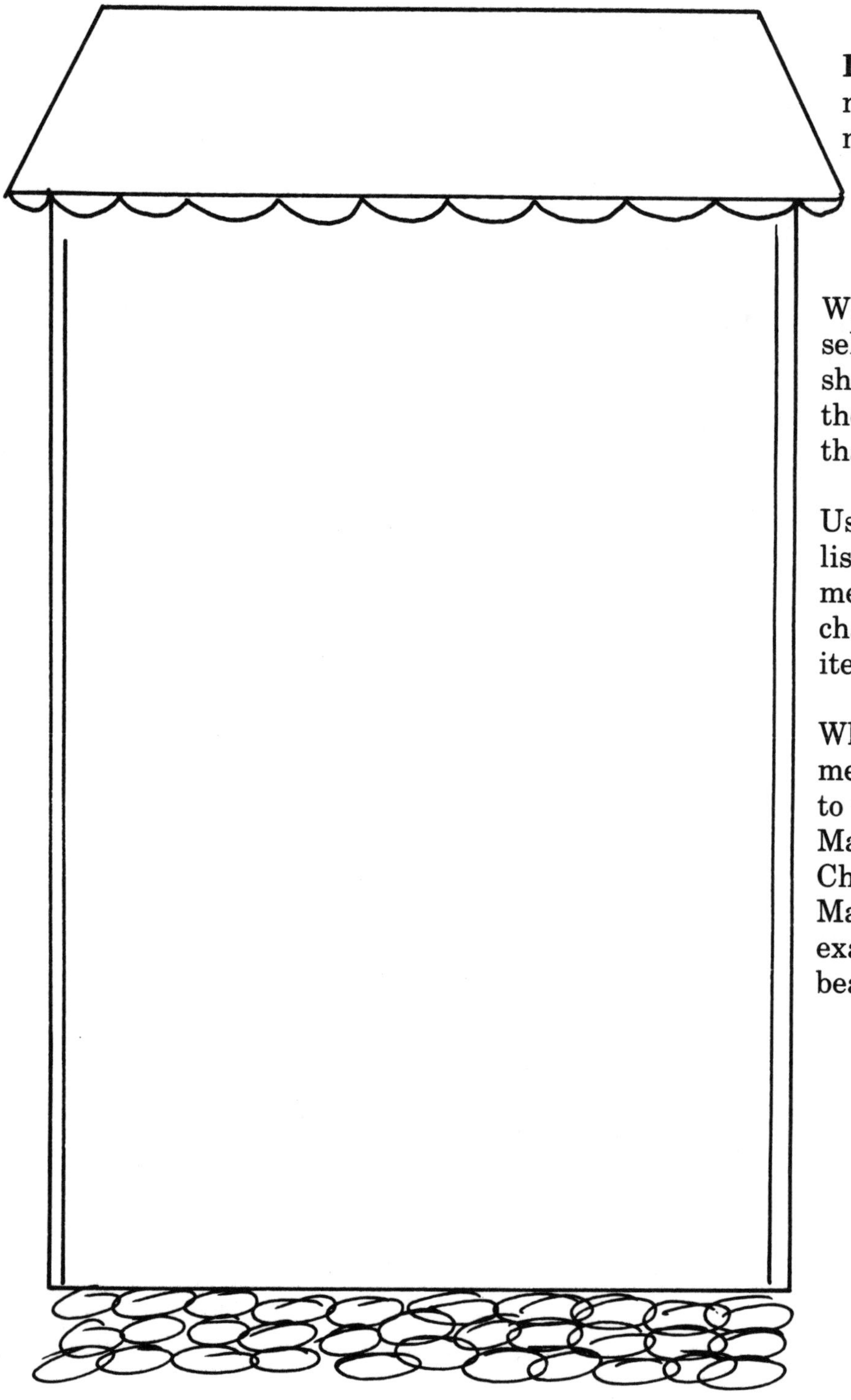

Directions: Create a new Market Street merchant!

What item is he or she selling? On a separate sheet of paper, list all the details that go with that item.

Use the details you have listed to create a new merchant. Draw the merchant and the detailed items in the shop.

What would your merchant be calling out to the shoppers on Market Street? Challenge yourself! Make it alliterative! For example, "Buy my beautifully bound books!"

© 1992 by The Center for Applied Research in Education

Name ______________________

ON MARKET STREET

IDEA SHEET 4–2

Directions: Think of four ways Market Street merchants can be successful (money, happiness, etc.). Put one idea in each of the small rectangles of the chart. For each idea, list in the corresponding larger rectangle the merchant you think will be the MOST successful and explain why. For example,

money	The book merchant will be most successful because he will probably sell all his books. Hard-cover books are expensive.

①	②

Which merchant do you think will be LEAST successful? Why?

© 1992 by The Center for Applied Research in Education

Name ____________________

ON MARKET STREET

IDEA SHEET 4–3

Directions: On the chart below, list ten good qualities of a friend. Think of the boy in the book *On Market Street.* For each quality you have listed, put an X in the YES box if he has that quality. Put an X in the CAN'T TELL box if it is not indicated. Use the ME column to rate yourself as a friend. What conclusions can you draw? How do you compare to the boy in the book?

GOOD QUALITIES OF A FRIEND	YES	CAN'T TELL	ME

© 1992 by The Center for Applied Research in Education

Name ______________________

ON MARKET STREET

IDEA SHEET 4–4

Directions: Describe what the different merchants would have to do to protect their merchandise in different kinds of weather.

IF THE WEATHER IS . . .	THE MERCHANTS HAVE TO . . .

© 1992 by The Center for Applied Research in Education

ON MARKET STREET

OPEN-ENDED IDEA SHEET

© 1992 by The Center for Applied Research in Education

"Winter Worlds"
by Ethel Jacobson

Our cedars are steeples of snow,
    Our shrubs are mounds of ice,
But under them, to and fro
    Go partridges and mice.

With crystal roofs and walls
    Their crisscrossed tunnels lead
To cozy dens and halls
    And storerooms stocked with winter feed.

What softly pattering feet
    Scurry unseen below
Our world of ice and sleet,
    Our land of steepled snow!

MY ILLUSTRATION

© 1992 by The Center for Applied Research in Education

"WINTER WORLDS"
by Ethel Jacobson
from Poetry Place Anthology

(New York: Instructor Books, 1983)

Language Arts Teaching Activities
Skills: Descriptive Language, Synonyms

- Using Idea Sheet 4–5, list the descriptive images of the poem: steeples of snow, mounds of ice, crystal roofs and walls, crisscrossed tunnels, cozy dens, and softly pattering feet. List synonyms that could be substituted for the adjectives.

- Divide the class into groups. Have the groups illustrate the descriptive phrases of the poem. Arrange the pictures to fit the sequence of the poem.
- Compose a free association poem for things that are crisscrossed, things that form mounds, things that are cozy, etc. For example,

Things that are criss-crossed

mazes · roads, tunnels. long. windy · dark. puzzling · mazes

- Consider the synonym substitutions for the descriptive phrases. Using the criteria of rhythm and image, which synonyms would be good to use? Which would you not recommend using?

Math Teaching Activities
Skill: Mazes

- Draw a picture of crisscrossed tunnels and dens for the bulletin board. Count the number of turns and dens. Measure the length of the straight areas.
- Compare sizes of burrowing animals and draw tunnels to scale for the different animals.
- Create a winter world maze that includes wrong turns and dead ends. Use Idea Sheet 4–6 to get the maze started.
- Collect several examples of mazes. Rank them in order of difficulty and explain your criteria.

Social Studies Teaching Activities
Skill: Geographical Areas

- Which parts of the world have climates like that described in the poem? Color code a map, and distinguish northern and southern hemispheres.
- Compare the hemispheres using international weather reports or the almanac. Which places do not have ice, snow, sleet? Graph the information.
- Change the poem so it describes animals that are active during the winter months.

- Use Idea Sheet 4–7 to survey classmates who have lived in different geographical areas. What were the seasons like? What did your classmates like and dislike about the area? List advantages and disadvantages of different climates.

Science Teaching Activities
Skill: Animals

- Identify animals that don't hibernate. Show them in a habitat web.

Pond — HABITATS — forest — raccoon
ducks
grasslands — deer
rabbit

- How do animals react to changes in the environment? Choose one animal and show its changes in a sequenced picture strip.
- Using Idea Sheet 4–8, compose humorous sayings the animals might think as the winter arrives. For example,

- Take the viewpoint of the animal. Describe one animal's life throughout the four seasons. Draw conclusions about the animal's life.

Name ______________________________

WINTER WORLDS

IDEA SHEET 4–5

Directions: Use a thesaurus to list synonyms for the underlined words in the descriptive images from the poem.

IMAGES	SYNONYMS
steeples of snow	mountains, buttes, ridges
mounds of ice	
crystal roofs and walls	
crisscrossed tunnels	
cozy dens	
softly pattering feet	

© 1992 by The Center for Applied Research in Education

Name ______________________________

WINTER WORLDS

IDEA SHEET 4–6

Directions: Create a winter worlds maze that includes wrong turns and dead ends.

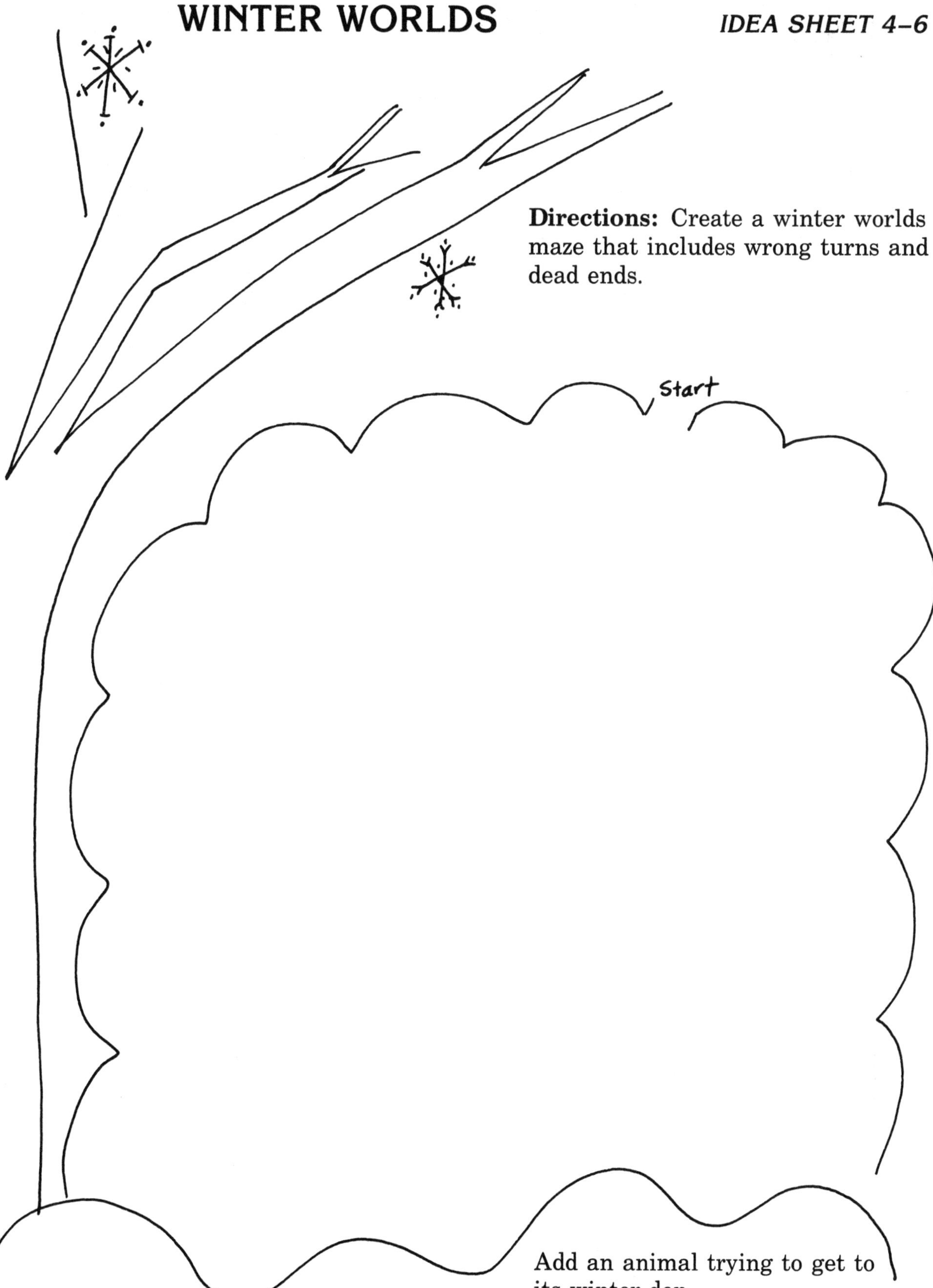

Add an animal trying to get to its winter den.

© 1992 by The Center for Applied Research in Education

Name ____________________

WINTER WORLDS

IDEA SHEET 4–7

Directions: Survey your friends. List the geographic areas in which they have lived and have them describe the seasons as mild, moderate, or hard. What did they like about the area? What did they dislike?

FRIEND	AREA/ SEASONS	LIKED	DISLIKED
Elliott Eskimo	Alaska - hard winter moderate spring mild summer moderate fall	lots of snow and ice for sledding	the short spring-summer-fall

© 1992 by The Center for Applied Research in Education

Name ______________________________

WINTER WORLDS

IDEA SHEET 4–8

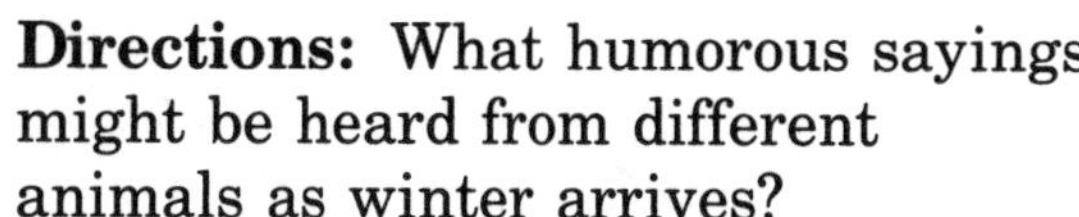

Directions: What humorous sayings might be heard from different animals as winter arrives?

ANIMAL	HUMOROUS QUOTE
mouse	"Thank goodness for my natural snow-toes!"

© 1992 by The Center for Applied Research in Education

WINTER WORLDS

OPEN-ENDED IDEA SHEET

© 1992 by The Center for Applied Research in Education

"This Little Light of Mine"
(Traditional Song)

This little light of mine,
I'm gonna let it shine,
This little light of mine,
I'm gonna let it shine,
This little light of mine,
I'm gonna let it shine,
Let it shine, let it shine, let it shine.

My brothers and my sisters, I'm gonna help them shine.
My brothers and my sisters, I'm gonna help them shine.
My brothers and my sisters, I'm gonna help them shine,
Help them shine, help them shine, help them shine.

This little love of ours, I'm gonna let it shine,
This little love of ours, I'm gonna let it shine,
This little love of ours, I'm gonna let it shine,
Let it shine, let it shine, let it shine.

This big world of ours, I'm gonna help it shine,
This big world of ours, I'm gonna help it shine,
This big world of ours, I'm gonna help it shine,
Help it shine, help it shine, help it shine.

MY ILLUSTRATION

© 1992 by The Center for Applied Research in Education

"This Little Light of Mine"
Traditional Song

© 1992 by The Center for Applied Research in Education

"THIS LITTLE LIGHT OF MINE"
(Traditional Song)

Language Arts Teaching Activities
Skill: Metaphors

- List lots of different light sources. Show these in a mobile.
- Make a checklist of the attributes of different light sources. For example,

Source	Attributes: intensity varies	natural	man-made	
lamp	✓		✓	
sun	✓	✓		

- Use Idea Sheet 4–9 to write a personal example of your shining light. For example,

  I become a shining light when I visit my grandmother and her friends at her retirement village.

- Write a personal explanation of why certain things may make your light shine, whereas other things make other people's lights shine.

Math Teaching Activities
Skills: Classification, Sets

- Make a collage of magazine pictures showing the different sets from the song.

  lights . . . brothers and sisters . . . love . . . the world

- Analyze the collage. How many pictures were found for each set? Which pictures might fit more than one set? Was there one set for which it was harder to find pictures? Why or why not? What other statements can be made about the collage?

- Think of a picture that would fit a set from the song that is *not* represented in the collage. Draw it.
- Choose the set you like best and explain why it's your favorite.

Social Studies Teaching Activities
Skill: Cooperation

- Invite guest speakers to discuss cooperation with students and show how cooperation leads to shining community efforts. Start with your principal, and expand to firefighters, police officers, service organizations, and charities. Summarize their ideas in a class book.
- Use Idea Sheet 4–10 to have students survey parents, siblings, and friends for examples of how people help others shine. Compare their findings. What conclusions can be drawn?
- Using Idea Sheet 4–11, have students design shining medals to keep in the classroom and award to especially helpful classmates.
- As a group, generate criteria for awarding the shining medals.

Science Teaching Activities
Skill: Ecology

- Make a display of articles, pictures, and personal observations about the environment and recycling.
- Consider your neighborhood. What examples of a shining world can be found? What areas can be targeted for clean-up?
- Design posters that promote taking care of the environment. Display them throughout your community.
- What are some practical suggestions children can follow to help our world shine? Record ideas on Idea Sheet 4–12. Evaluate which could be group efforts, individual efforts, school efforts, and community efforts.

Name ____________________

THIS LITTLE LIGHT OF MINE

IDEA SHEET 4–9

Directions: Think about how you shine like a light when you do something well or when you do something for others. Write a personal example of your shining light.

© 1992 by The Center for Applied Research in Education

Name ______________________

THIS LITTLE LIGHT OF MINE

IDEA SHEET 4–10

Directions: Survey family members and friends to find out how people help others shine. Bring your information to school to compare with others.

I interviewed ________, and he/she said...

I asked ________,
and he/she said...

I talked with ________,
and he/she said...

© 1992 by The Center for Applied Research in Education

Name ______________________________

THIS LITTLE LIGHT OF MINE

IDEA SHEET 4–11

Directions: Design shining medals to use as awards. Brainstorm phrases to put on the medals. Decorate each medal for a different purpose. Cut them out and mount on construction paper or foil. Watch for deserving recipients!

Phrases I might use:

____

____

____

____

____

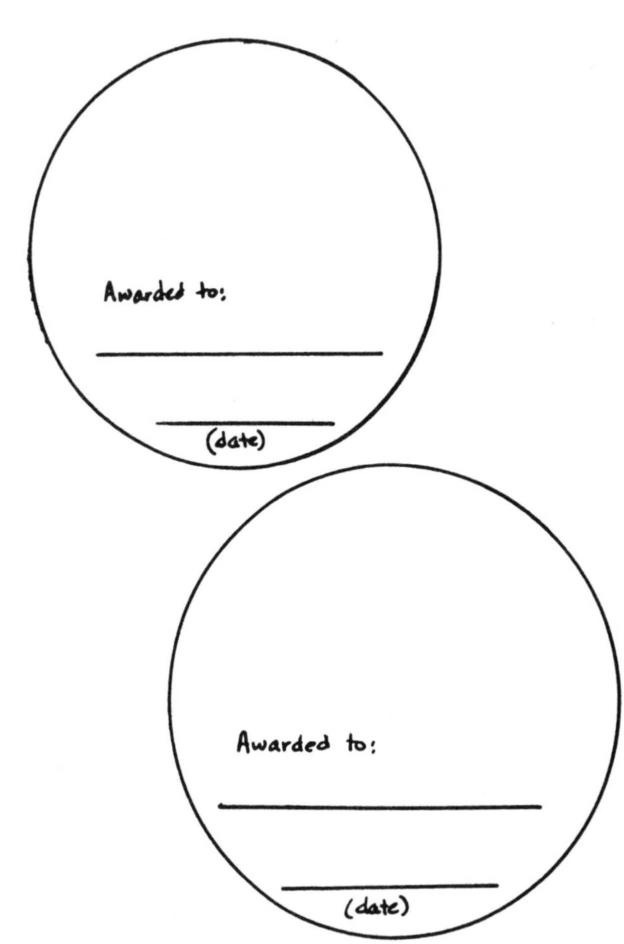

© 1992 by The Center for Applied Research in Education

Name ______________________

THIS LITTLE LIGHT OF MINE

IDEA SHEET 4–12

Directions: On the globe, write some practical examples to help our world shine. Code them: G = Group effort, S = School effort, C = Community effort.

For example: We can recycle glass, paper, and aluminum.
G, S, C

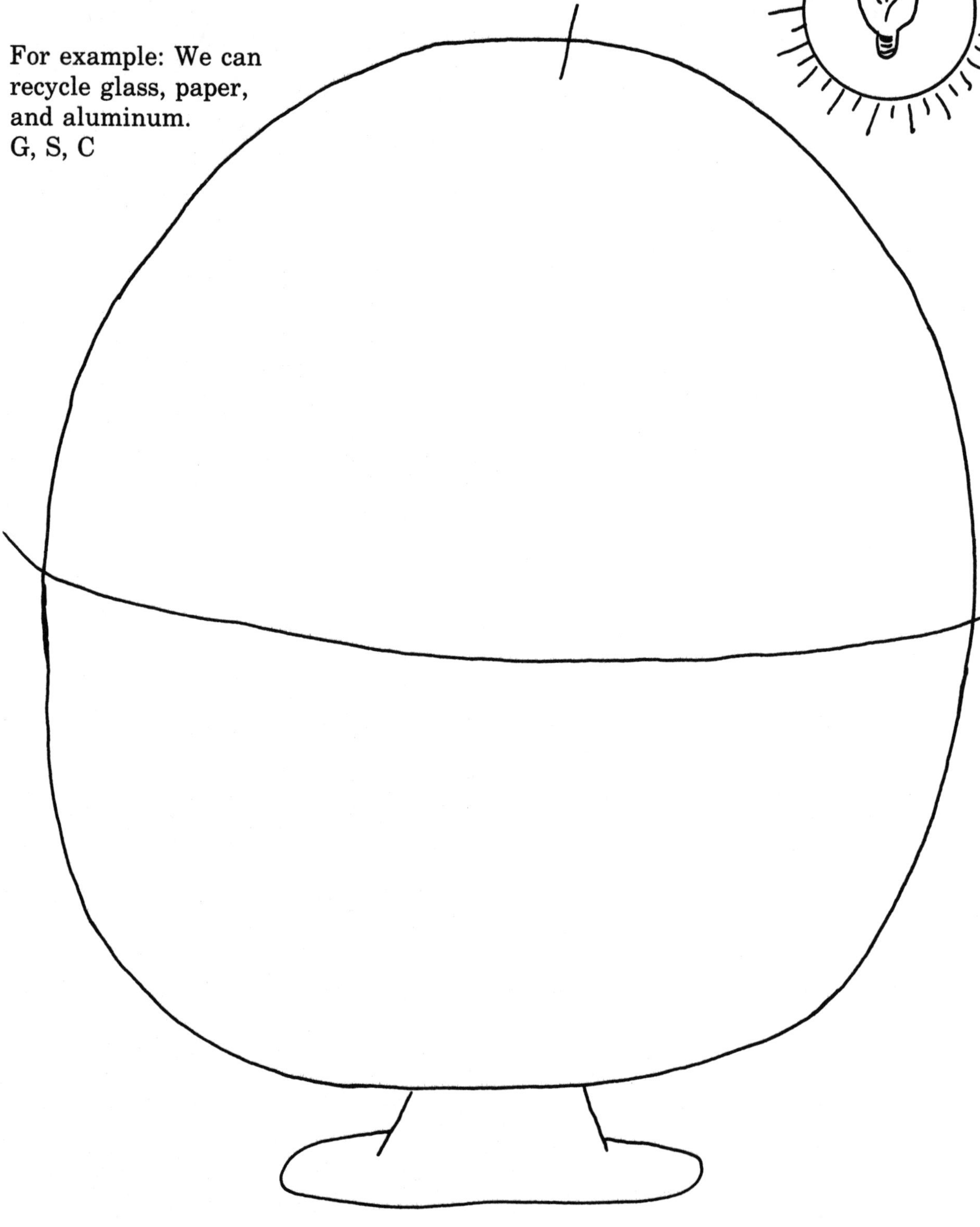

© 1992 by The Center for Applied Research in Education

THIS LITTLE LIGHT OF MINE

OPEN-ENDED IDEA SHEET

© 1992 by The Center for Applied Research in Education

5

January

OWL MOON
by Jane Yolen
Illustrated by John Schoenherr
(New York: Philomel Books, 1987)
Caldecott Medal Winner, 1988

A young girl and her father take an "owling" walk on a winter's moonlit evening. The hush of the still night setting combines with soft descriptions to create a vivid mood for the reader. The reader delights in sharing the companionship of the father and daughter in their unusual adventure.

Language Arts Teaching Activities
Skills: Characterization, Illustrations, Format

- Consider the two characters in the story and list their attributes in a chart or on large silhouettes of the characters. For example,

Character	attributes
Father	quiet, strong

- Use Idea Sheet 5–1 to web how the format of the book helps relay information about winter and the girl's adventure. Consider the illustrations and text. Are the illustrations realistic? detailed? How does the text add factual information?

Colors show winter cold — illustrations — text — "feet crunched over crisp snow"

- Enjoy experimenting with watercolors to achieve the same artistic style as the book. Plan a promotional party for the book that includes banners, bookmarks, posters, etc. Include information about the book on the products you make.
- Imagine that you are on the Caldecott Award Committee. Role-play a discussion of the merits of *Owl Moon.* Defend why it deserves the Caldecott Medal.

Math Teaching Activities
Skills: Math Concepts, Time

- On Idea Sheet 5–2, identify concepts that a mathematician might notice in the book. For example, noticing long and short things, counting objects, looking for patterns (footprints, text), noting the use of time.
- How does the text show that the girl lost track of time? Generate other examples of how people lose track of time.

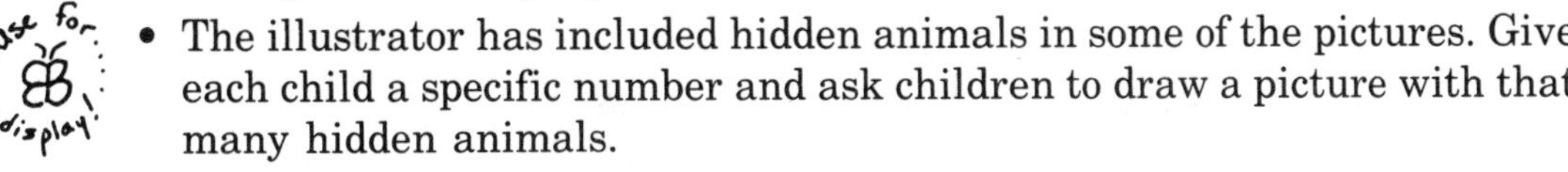

- The illustrator has included hidden animals in some of the pictures. Give each child a specific number and ask children to draw a picture with that many hidden animals.
- The total number of pages in picture books is always a multiple of eight. Does this book fit that criterion? Judge the placement of the illustrations with the text. Are there any parts that have been extended or compacted?

Social Studies Teaching Activities
Skill: Families

- *Owl Moon* was written from the author's personal family experience. What other books can you find that could have been written from personal experience?

- Discuss the information on the book jacket flap regarding the author's personal experiences with "owling." What other means besides writing books do people use for saving personal experiences? List your ideas in a flyer.

- Paint a picture of an experience your family shared.
- Families are groups of individuals that enjoy a variety of activities. Use Idea Sheet 5–3 to list reasons why some events and activities are "group" and some are "individual." Compose a manners guide for family activities.

Science Teaching Activities
Skill: Owls

- Imitate the great horned owl sound described in the story. Read the story and imitate the sounds of the hidden animals as they appear in the book. Focus on the owl to complete the following chart.

Attributes:	feathers	talons	big eyes	beak
Use of attributes:	to fly protection from weather	strong grip for hunting	night sight	feeding

- What else would you like to know about the owl? Using Idea Sheet 5–4, start a set of owl cards listing facts about the owl that can be derived from the book. Research additional facts to list on additional cards. Devise games to go with the set of cards.
- Evaluate using this book to learn about owls as compared to a completely factual source. What differences do you notice? How might a personal story add to information? How does it detract from information? What personal story could you write that would incorporate factual information?

Name ______________________________

IDEA SHEET 5–1

Directions: Web how the format of the book helps relay information about winter and the girl's adventure.

© 1992 by The Center for Applied Research in Education

Name ____________________

IDEA SHEET 5–2

Directions: Think about the story from a math point of view. List things from the book that would fit these sets.

LONG/SHORT THINGS

THINGS TO COUNT

PATTERNS

TIME

© 1992 by The Center for Applied Research in Education

Name ______________________________

IDEA SHEET 5–3

Directions:
Families are groups of individuals who enjoy doing things together or on their own. What makes an activity something for individuals to do together? alone? What manners are important for group activities? Use this sheet to list your ideas.

REASONS TO DO SOMETHING TOGETHER

REASONS TO DO SOMETHING ALONE

MANNERS THAT ARE IMPORTANT FOR GROUP ACTIVITIES

© 1992 by The Center for Applied Research in Education

OWL MOON

Name ______________________

IDEA SHEET 5–4

Directions: Make a set of owl fact cards by listing one fact on each owl card and cutting out each card. Research owls and add more cards to the set. Create a game to go with your cards.

Owl Facts

Owls answer each other's calls.

Owl Facts

Owl Facts

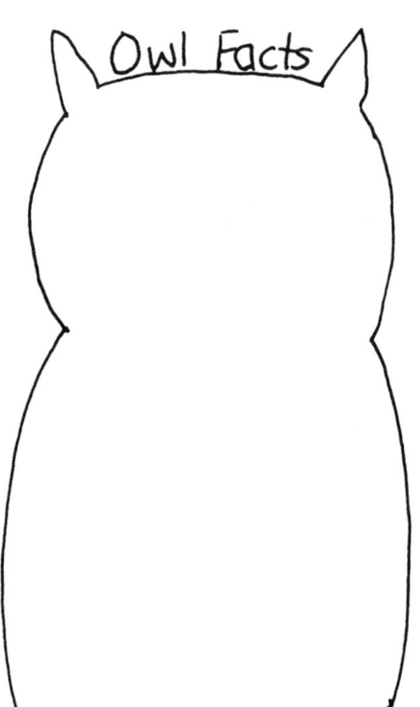

© 1992 by The Center for Applied Research in Education

OPEN-ENDED IDEA SHEET

© 1992 by The Center for Applied Research in Education

"The New Year"
by Margaret Oleson

A glad New Year, each day a page,
    As fresh and white as snow;
Cold winter, and waking spring,
    And summer, warm and slow;
Bright autumn, jolly Halloween,
    Thanksgiving, Christmas cheer–
The record of a happy time,
    A beautiful New Year!

MY ILLUSTRATION

© 1992 by The Center for Applied Research in Education

"THE NEW YEAR"
by Margaret Oleson
from Poetry Place Anthology

(New York: Instructor Books, 1983)

Language Arts Teaching Activities
Skill: Cyclical Poems and Stories

- Using Idea Sheet 5–5, chart how the poem cycles through the seasons. Add special days that have not been included.
- Compare this poem with other forms of literature that "cycle," such as
  - *If You Give a Mouse a Cookie,* by Laura Joffe Numeroff, Scholastic, 1985.
  - *The Ox-Cart Man,* by Donald Hall, Puffin Books, 1988. **Note:** See October section for teaching activities.
  - *The Ernie and Bert Book,* featuring Jim Henson's Sesame Street Muppets, Golden Press, 1977.
- Write your own cycle poem or story.
- Which cycle stories did you like best? Why?

Math Teaching Activities
Skill: Calendars

- Collect facts about calendars.
- Compare different kinds of calendars: lunar, ancient, modern.
- Make a calendar for this year and note personal events to remember.
- Evaluate different ways of keeping track of time and events (clocks, diaries, logs, etc.). Using Idea Sheet 5–6, survey people to find out their methods of time keeping. What conclusions can be drawn?

Social Studies Teaching Activities
Skill: Holiday Celebrations

- Research multicultural and unfamiliar holidays such as the following: (**Note:** The dates of the holidays with blank spaces vary slightly from year to year.)

September
____ Ethiopia's New Year
____ Rosh Hashanah (Jewish New Year)
____ Divali, India

October
1st Monday–Universal Children's Day
9 Leif Ericson Day, Norway
15 Confucius Day, China
24 United Nations Day

November
11 St. Martin's Day, European countries
____ Festival of Climbing the Heights, China
15 7-5-3 Festival, Japan
25 St. Catherine's Day, France

December
12 Feast of Our Lady of Guadalupe, Mexico
____ Hanukkah
13 St. Lucia's Day, Sweden
15 Navidades, Puerto Rico
16 Posadas, Mexico
19 St. Nicholas Day, Russian Orthodox
____ Winter Solstice

January
____ Chinese New Year
____ Tet, Vietnam (first seven days of first month of lunar calendar)

February
____ Brotherhood Week
____ Shrove Tuesday
____ Fasching, Germany

March
3 Girls Day, Japan–Feast of Dolls
5 Boys Day, Japan
13–19 Festival of St. Joseph, Valencia, Spain

April
2 Hans Christian Andersen Day, Denmark
8 Buddha's Birthday
13 Water Festival, Thailand
23 Children's Day, Turkey

May
1 International Labor Day
5 Children's Day, Japan
5 Cinco de Mayo, Mexico

13 Joan of Arc Day, France
25 Youth Day, Yugoslavia

June
11 Kamehanmehe Day, Hawaii
18 International Picnic Day

July
4 Friendship Day
14 Bastille Day, France

August
13 Fox Hill Day, Bahamas
15 Sour Herring Premiere, Sweden

- What holidays are celebrated in your area that could be inserted into the poem? For example, "festive Tet."
- Use Idea Sheet 5–7 to create a holiday that would be particular to your school.
- Invite children's recommendations for class holiday celebrations. Set criteria for judging ideas. Examples: Be sensitive to everyone's beliefs; activities must fit within the time frame; activities must include everyone. Incorporate ideas into your next celebration.

Science Teaching Activities
Skill: Yearly Changes

- Consider the school year cycle. Use Idea Sheet 5–8 to chart the changes you anticipate such as seasonal changes, changes in things we use, changes in things we study, etc.
- Compare your chart with a friend's. Add items to your list that are new.
- Think of effects the expected changes will have and add them to Idea Sheet 5–8.
- Evaluate the anticipated effects. From your viewpoint, what impact will the effects have on you, your parents, or your school? Which changes would you welcome or plan to avoid?

Name ______________________________

THE NEW YEAR

IDEA SHEET 5–5

Directions: The poem "The New Year" highlights the following special characteristics of the seasons. Add your own ideas of special events to the list.

new year
snow

waking plants and animals

bright autumn colors
Thanksgiving

warm, slow days

© 1992 by The Center for Applied Research in Education

Name ______________________

THE NEW YEAR

IDEA SHEET 5–6

Directions: Survey how people keep track of time. Record their names above the methods they use. What conclusions can you make?

PEOPLE SURVEYED					
9					
8					
7					
6					
5					
4					
3					
2					
1					
	CLOCK	DAILY SCHEDULE	ROUTINE	OTHER	OTHER

WAYS OF KEEPING TRACK OF TIME

Conclusions: ____

____

____

____

____

____

____

© 1992 by The Center for Applied Research in Education

Name ______________________

THE NEW YEAR

IDEA SHEET 5–7

Directions: The poem "The New Year" highlights special times throughout the seasons. Create a holiday that would be particular to your school. Generate ideas by listing special features of your school.

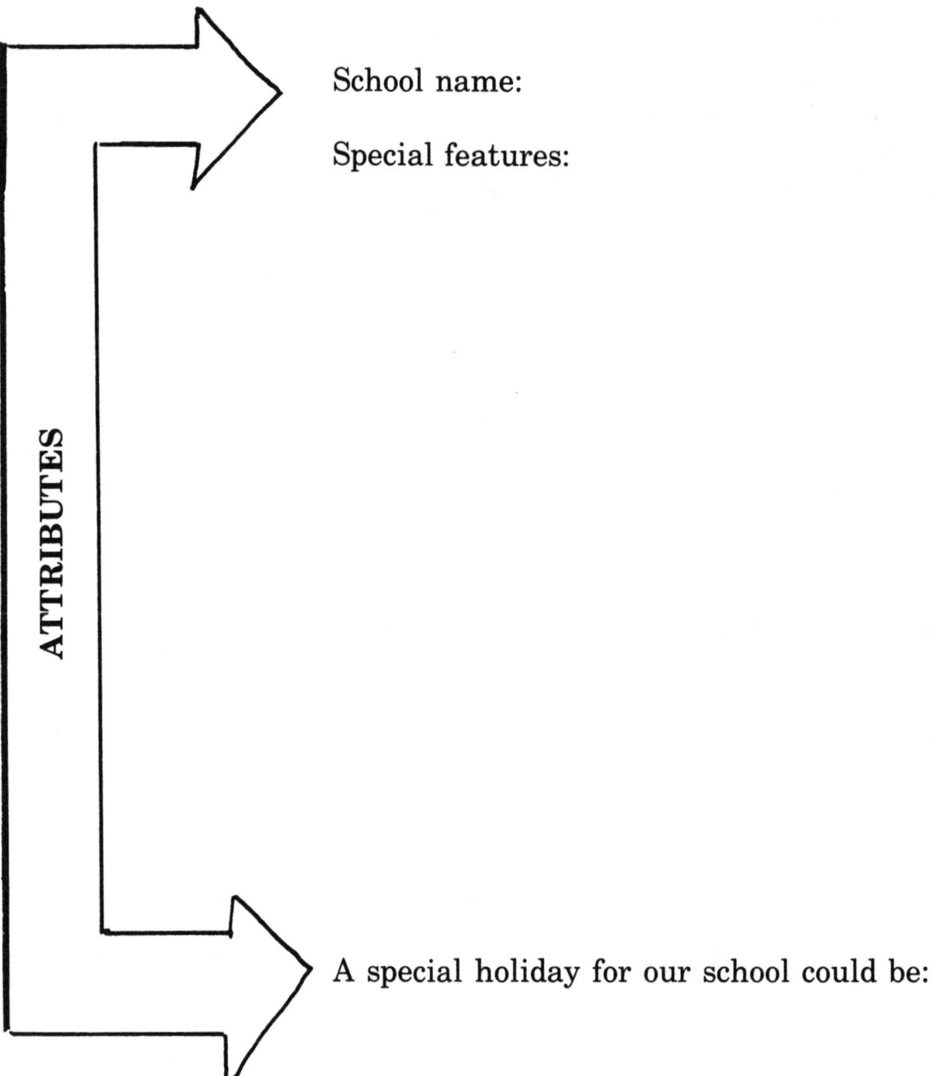

© 1992 by The Center for Applied Research in Education

Name ____________________

THE NEW YEAR

IDEA SHEET 5–8

Directions: Chart the changes you expect throughout the school year.

ANTICIPATED CHANGES	EFFECTS	MY REACTIONS
Example: The weather will change.	People will wear different kinds of clothes.	It will be fun to switch clothes.

© 1992 by The Center for Applied Research in Education

THE NEW YEAR

OPEN-ENDED IDEA SHEET

© 1992 by The Center for Applied Research in Education

"If You're Happy and You Know It"
(Traditional Song)

If you're happy and you know it, clap your hands,
If you're happy and you know it, clap your hands,
If you're happy and you know it,
then your face will surely show it,
If you're happy and you know it, clap your hands.

If you're happy and you know it, tap your toe,
If you're happy and you know it, tap your toe,
If you're happy and you know it,
then your face will surely show it,
If you're happy and you know it, tap your toe.

If you're happy and you know it, nod your head,
If you're happy and you know it, nod your head,
If you're happy and you know it,
then your face will surely show it,
If you're happy and you know it, nod your head.

MY ILLUSTRATION

© 1992 by The Center for Applied Research in Education

"If You're Happy and You Know It"
Traditional Song

© 1992 by The Center for Applied Research in Education

"IF YOU'RE HAPPY AND YOU KNOW IT"
(Traditional Song)

Language Arts Teaching Activities
Skill: Dramatics

- Make paper-plate masks of different living things, book characters, or people to illustrate all the possible subjects of this song.

Idea! Mount the paper plate mask on a strip of paper and wear it as a hat-mask.

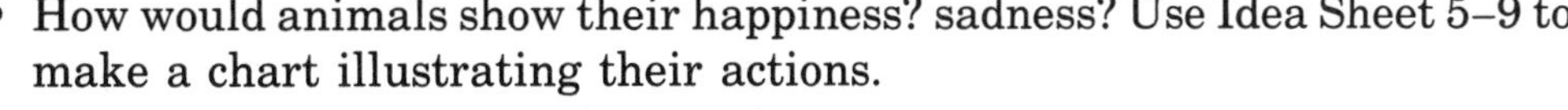

- How would animals show their happiness? sadness? Use Idea Sheet 5–9 to make a chart illustrating their actions.

- Compose different verses for animals and book characters. Assign them to individuals or buddies to act out as the class sings the new verses. Prepare a final verse to sum up the entire song. For example:

Stanzas:

> If a pup is happy and he knows it, he wags his tail,
> If Corduroy is happy and he knows it,
> he'll give you a hug,

Final verse:

> When they're happy and they know it, you will
> see them show it!

- Have students compose a journal entry telling in what ways this song could be helpful.

Math Teaching Activities
Skill: If . . . Then Logic Statements

- Using Idea Sheet 5–10, ask students to complete logic statements for themselves.
- Compare everyone's logic statements. Graph the results. What commonalities and differences are there?

- Make a set of cards with a different feeling on each one: happy, sad, silly, clever, full, hungry, athletic, etc. Have children choose cards and write if . . . then statements for each one. Illustrate them.
- Divide the class into small groups to compose if . . . then statements for different occupations. As they share their ideas, have them explain their if . . . then statements. For example,

Teacher	If the students are working quietly, then the teacher is happy because she can conference students without interruptions.
Mail carrier	If ______________________________,
	then ______________________________.

Social Studies Teaching Activities
Skill: Feelings

- Make a long list of all the feelings that could fit in the song. On a string of cut-out people or Idea Sheet 5–11, show different faces depicting the feelings. Substitute the different feelings into the song.

- How would the response change for each of the new emotions? List a new response on each cut-out figure.
- Make a graffiti board on which students list all the things that would make them happy, sad, etc.

- Evaluate the graffiti board from different viewpoints. Which things could apply to the principal? a friend? a pet? a parent?

Science Teaching Activities
Skill: Weather

- Think of different weather conditions that could fit the tune of the song. Record ideas on Idea Sheet 5–12. Consider displaying some of the ideas on large cut-out shapes.
- Analyze the clothes that would be necessary for the different weather situations. Add verses showing these connections:

  If it's __________ and you know it, what would you wear?
  If it's raining and you know it, put on your boots.

  Or try the inverse!

  If you have on your boots and a raincoat, what's the weather?

- Make up your own weather song to a familiar tune.
- What rhythm instruments and motions would enhance the song? the new verses? In what way are they an improvement?

Name ______________________

IDEA SHEET 5–9

If You're Happy and You Know It...

Directions: Think about animals. How do they show their happiness? sadness? Make a chart showing animals' feelings and actions.

ANIMAL	EMOTION	ACTION
puppy	happy	wags its tail

© 1992 by The Center for Applied Research in Education

Name ______________________

IDEA SHEET 5–10

Directions: What makes you happy? How do you show you're happy? Think of several examples of things that make you happy and how you react to those specific examples. Write them in an if . . . then pattern.

For example,

If ___there's ice cream for a treat___,

then I'm happy and ___I say, "Oh, yummy!"___.

If ______________________________

______________________________,

then I'm happy and ______________________________

______________________________.

If ______________________________

______________________________,

then I'm happy and ______________________________

______________________________.

If ______________________________

______________________________,

then I'm happy and ______________________________

______________________________.

© 1992 by The Center for Applied Research in Education

Name ______________________

IDEA SHEET 5–11

Directions: What other feelings could fit this song? How would the verses change? List new feelings, show a matching expression on the face circle, and add an action for a new verse.

If you're ____sad____ and you feel it,

____then say boo-hoo____.

If you're ______________ and you feel it,

______________________.

If you're ______________ and you feel it,

______________________.

If you're ______________ and you feel it,

______________________.

© 1992 by The Center for Applied Research in Education

Name ____________________

IDEA SHEET 5–12

If You're Happy and You Know It...

Directions: Think of different weather conditions that could fit the tune of this song. What action would go with the different types of weather? Fill in the blanks for a weather song!

ILLUSTRATIONS	WEATHER VERSES
	Example: If it's raining and you know it, cover your head!
	If it's ____________ and you know it, ______________________!
	If it's ____________ and you know it, ______________________!
	If it's ____________ and you know it, ______________________!

© 1992 by The Center for Applied Research in Education

OPEN-ENDED IDEA SHEET

If You're Happy and You Know It . . .

© 1992 by The Center for Applied Research in Education

6

February

A CHAIR FOR MY MOTHER
by Vera B. Williams

(New York: Mulberry Books, 1982)
Caldecott Honor Book, 1983

This is a story of a mother, daughter, and grandmother whose family and neighbors help them set up an apartment after their home is destroyed by a fire. The mother, a waitress in a diner, saves all her tips in a big money jar in order to buy a comfortable chair to put by the window. When the jar is finally full, the mother, grandmother, and daughter go shopping and find a "wonderful, beautiful, fat, soft armchair" that is a dream come true.

Language Arts Teaching Activities
Skill: Characterizations

- How is this little girl's life like yours? Paint a watercolor picture of some aspect of her life that is the same as yours.
- Look carefully at the borders of each page in the story. Describe how they correspond to the mood and events happening in the story at that point. Design a border for a picture about your life.
- Compose a class story. Have everyone illustrate a different page. Draw borders for each page to match the story event and mood.

- Evaluate how other people could react to this book. What would ________ say about the story? Why? Role-play a child, a mother, a teacher, a store manager, a waitress, etc. Use Idea Sheet 6–1 as a follow-up to this group activity.

Math Teaching Activities
Skill: Money

- Start a jar of play money in your classroom. Students earn money for specific tasks and behaviors, and they contribute their earnings to the jar. The class can earn money toward a new book or game for the classroom. How long does it take to reach a goal?
- In shopping for the chair, the little girl, her mother, and her grandmother tried lots of chairs. They identified a need and considered specific attributes. Together with your students, identify a classroom need, list specific attributes, and then provide catalogs for children to "comparison shop" for similar items. Have a discussion about the "best buy."
- Invite a guest speaker from a bank to share consumer information with the class.
- Create a set of class money. Set up a class bank with a special location, specific hours of operation, employees' job descriptions, etc. Use this special money for the play money activity explained above.
- In the book, Grandma got a bargain on tomatoes and bananas. Use Idea Sheet 6–2 to define and discuss the idea of a bargain. Incorporate newspaper grocery ads as references, and list things to remember when looking for a bargain. Publish the list for "shoppers" to use.

Social Studies Teaching Activities
Skill: Families

- Using Idea Sheet 6–3, identify different family groups. For the bulletin board, draw an apartment building with large windows. Have children illustrate different family combinations in each window of the building. Start with the family in the story.
- In the story, the little girl, her mother, and the grandmother depend on extended family members for help. Survey classmates to identify who has extended family with whom they share activities or responsibilities.
- Draw photos of your family and compose a photo essay of a big event your family has experienced.
- This story depicts how families help each other in times of need. List other examples of times of need. Make a chart or a web to show what causes these situations. How else do people help each other? Does your school have a community need that students could help solve?

Science Teaching Activities
Skills: Five Senses, Volume

- Consider the volume of the jar the family used. What other things besides coins could be measured with a jar? Make a long list of places in which you might look for a large jar.
- This story appeals to the five senses. Have the children work with a buddy to analyze a page and chart how it involves the senses. Students may then share ideas and compile results on Idea Sheet 6–4. Do you think the author deliberately tried to appeal to the senses? Why or why not?

- Collect a variety of jars. Consider their various attributes. Create different jar designs that would indicate their function as a money jar.
- Evaluate all the effects of a fire. Consider the viewpoints of a family, the neighbors, the firefighters, the neighborhood pets, etc. Show your ideas on a graffiti chart.

Name ______________________

A CHAIR FOR MY MOTHER

IDEA SHEET 6–1

How did you feel about this book?

Now write mini book reviews from other viewpoints—a mother, a waitress, a store manager, a furniture salesperson, an insurance salesperson, a neighbor, the author . . .

© 1992 by The Center for Applied Research in Education

SALE!

BARGAIN!

Name ____________________

A CHAIR FOR MY MOTHER

IDEA SHEET 6–2

Directions: Survey friends and relatives to find out everything you can about shopping for bargains. After you have listened to everybody else's ideas, write down what you think about bargains.

A bargain is . . .

It's not a bargain if . . .

The most important thing to remember is . . .

BARGAIN!

SALE!

© 1992 by The Center for Applied Research in Education

Name ______________________

A CHAIR FOR MY MOTHER

IDEA SHEET 6–3

Directions: Draw pictures that look like photographs in a picture album.

Here are family members who live with me:

Here are family members who live nearby:

Here are family members who live far away:

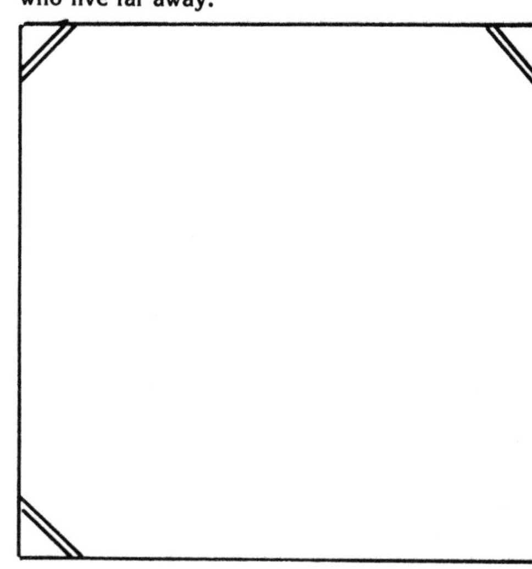

(Add another family category)

© 1992 by The Center for Applied Research in Education

Name ______________________

A CHAIR FOR MY MOTHER

IDEA SHEET 6–4

Directions: Write evidence of the five senses from at least three pages of the book. Leave the box blank if there is no evidence of that sense. Compare your ideas with a friend!

	SEEING	HEARING	SMELLING	TOUCHING	TASTING
pg.1	blue TV	"Good work, honey."	pepper, ketchup onions	money in jar	food at the diner

© 1992 by The Center for Applied Research in Education

A CHAIR FOR MY MOTHER

OPEN-ENDED IDEA SHEET

© 1992 by The Center for Applied Research in Education

"Dreams"
by Langston Hughes

Hold fast to dreams
For if dreams die
Life is a broken-winged bird
That cannot fly.

Hold fast to dreams
For when dreams go
Life is a barren field
Frozen with snow.

MY ILLUSTRATION

© 1992 by The Center for Applied Research in Education

"DREAMS"
by Langston Hughes
from Poetry Place Anthology

(New York: Instructor Books, 1983)

Language Arts Teaching Activities
Skill: Application

- Dreams are goals. Using Idea Sheet 6–5, describe a dream you might have for yourself, your country, and the world. Put possible obstacles aside and let your imagination soar!
- Choose one of the dreams described from the previous idea and list the steps that would be necessary to accomplish the dream.
- Paint a large picture depicting your dream.
- Rate the difficulty of accomplishing your dream by considering the time, the materials, and the assistance that would be needed. On a scale of 1 to 10 (1 = little, 10 = a lot), how does your dream rate? What advice might you have for yourself?

Math Teaching Activities
Skill: Number Patterns

- Consider the number pattern people create when they spread ideas and dreams: One person tells one person, then two know about the idea. Two people each tell another person, then four know about the idea. If you continued this pattern with the number of students in your classroom, how many people would know about the dream?
- What examples of community effort in your area reflect the pattern in the preceding activity? What problems in your community might be resolved if different service groups coordinated efforts? Categorize your community's needs by the number of groups needed to work together on the problem. For example,

  Adopt a Highway Program: One business or other group takes responsibility for cleaning up every 2 miles of assigned highway.

  Our area has

  ________ miles of community roads.

  Our community would need the support of ________ groups.

- Use geometric shapes to create a mathematical design that shows how this community problem-solving process builds wide involvement.

1, 2, 4, 8, 16, etc.

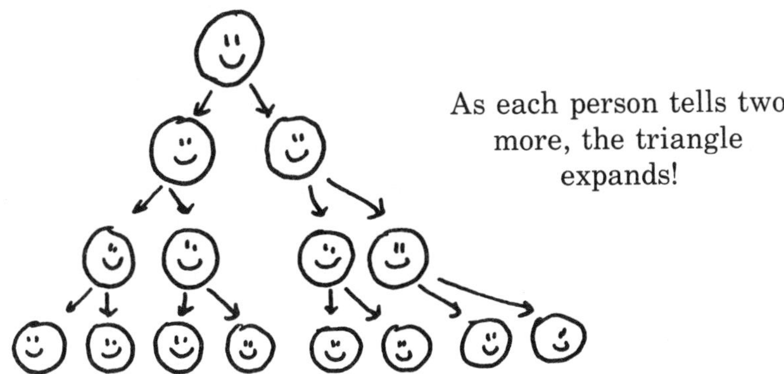

As each person tells two more, the triangle expands!

- What types of obstacles might be encountered with community problem solving? Use Idea Sheet 6–6 to organize your ideas. Compose a supportive editorial that contains logical statements showing how obstacles can be overcome. For example,

If we were to have bad weather on a community clean-up day,
then we would encourage participants to dress appropriately and still help out!

Social Studies Teaching Activities
Skill: Brotherhood

- Martin Luther King, Jr.'s dream was world brotherhood. Compose a resolution for school brotherhood and share it with your principal.
- Compare Martin Luther King, Jr.'s speech, "I Have a Dream," with Langston Hughes's poem. Use the Venn diagram on Idea Sheet 6–7 to show similarities and differences.

- Publish "school spirit" booklets or posters to promote a brotherhood goal for your school. Share them with other classes.
- Write questions to use in evaluating how well the school brotherhood goals are being implemented. Answer them as a self-inventory, and plan how to improve your efforts. For example,

Do I try to play with everyone?
Do I offer to help those who have a question?

Science Teaching Activities
Skill: Ecology

- Protecting the ecology of the earth is a dream of many people. Collect newspaper articles and group reports of efforts in your community to preserve the environment. Display them in a collage.
- Display a world map and collect articles about ecological efforts beyond your community. On the map, find the locations of these efforts. Categorize the efforts. Which areas have recycling facilities? Do any have regularly scheduled clean-up days? What legislative action has taken place?

- Create your own T-shirt design promoting ecology.
- Evaluate your own efforts toward ecology using Idea Sheet 6–8. Assess your daily, weekly, monthly, and yearly ecological efforts. What recommendations would you make to yourself?

Name ____________________

Dreams

IDEA SHEET 6–5

Directions: Dreams are goals. Describe a dream you might have for yourself, your country, and the world.

My dream for myself . . .

My dream for my country . . .

My dream for the world . . .

BONUS CHALLENGE! Choose one of your dreams and, on the back of this sheet, describe the steps necessary to accomplish that dream.

© 1992 by The Center for Applied Research in Education

Name ______________________________

Dreams

IDEA SHEET 6–6

Directions: What difficulties might occur when a community works together to solve a problem? Think of a community problem and steps to solve it. Then think of difficulties that might occur. Finally, write an editorial that contains logical statements showing how the difficulties could be overcome.

Community Problem:

Steps to Solve It:

Difficulties:

Editorial:

© 1992 by The Center for Applied Research in Education

Name ______________________

Dreams

IDEA SHEET 6–7

Directions: Compare Martin Luther King, Jr.'s speech, "I Have a Dream," with Langston Hughes's poem, "Dreams." List attributes particular to each on the appropriate side of the Venn diagram. List similarities in the middle.

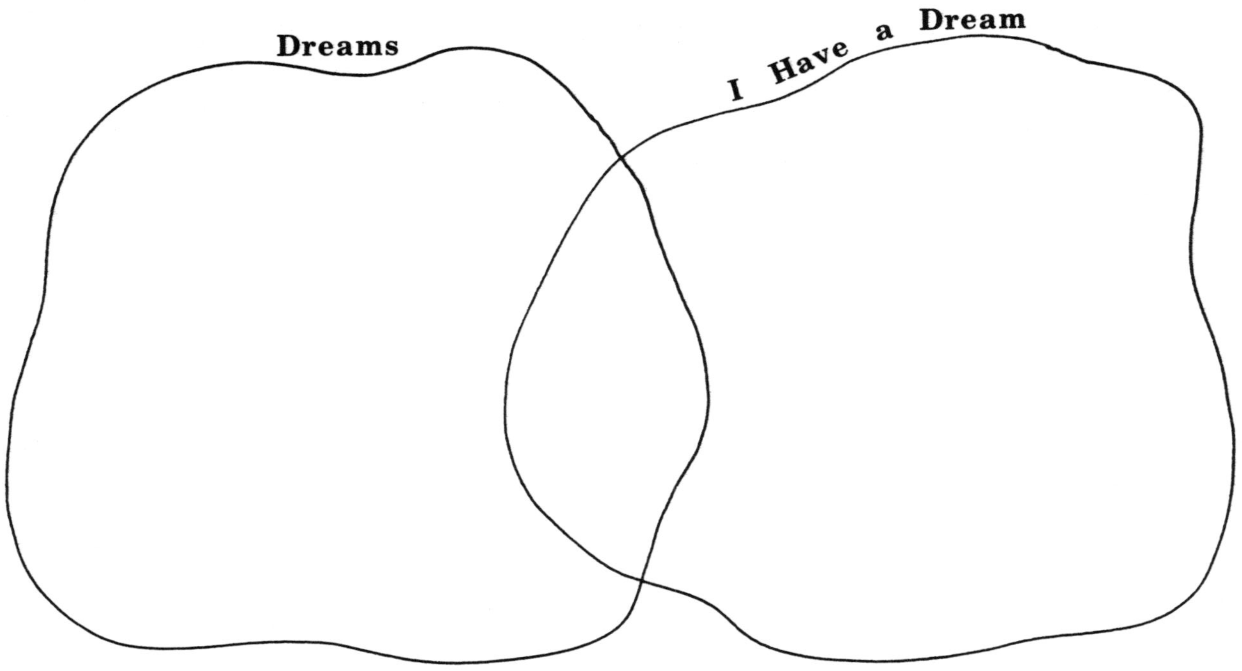

Dreams

I Have a Dream

© 1992 by The Center for Applied Research in Education

Name ______________________________

Dreams

IDEA SHEET 6–8

Directions: Evaluate yourself. List your daily, weekly, monthly, and yearly efforts toward ecology. What recommendations would you make to yourself?

DAILY

WEEKLY

MONTHLY

YEARLY

MY RECOMMENDATIONS TO MYSELF:

© 1992 by The Center for Applied Research in Education

© 1992 by The Center for Applied Research in Education

"Magic Penny"
by Malvina Reynolds

Love is something if you give it away,
give it away, give it away.
Love is something if you give it away,
You end up having more.

Oh, it's just like a magic penny:
hold it tight and you won't have any,
Lend it, spend it and you'll have so many,
they'll roll all over the floor; for

Love is something if you give it away,
give it away, give it away.
Love is something if you give it away,
You end up having more.

So let's go dancing til the break of day,
and if there's a piper, we can pay,
For love is something if you give it away,
you end up having more.

© 1992 by The Center for Applied Research in Education

MY ILLUSTRATION

"Magic Penny"
by Malvina Reynolds

© 1992 by The Center for Applied Research in Education

©1955, 1959 by Northern Music Company

"MAGIC PENNY"
by Malvina Reynolds

Language Arts Teaching Activities
Skill: Imagery

- Think of the different ways people show their love for each other. What actions show that we "give it away"? Web your ideas.
- Compare the loving care given by your family, friends, acquaintances, and distant relatives in the chart on Idea Sheet 6–9. What similarities and differences are there in their actions?
- Consider the line "it's just like a magic penny." Write or draw other things that could be compared in a simile with love. Use ideas from previous activities as a way to start your thinking. For example, "Love is like a shining star."
- Do you agree with the songwriter? Is love like a magic penny? Or do you prefer another simile? Support your opinion in a writing or roundtable discussion.

Math Teaching Activities
Skill: Money

- Collect pennies from around the world and display them for students to examine.
- Make penny cards to compare the different pennies. Record their sizes, markings, and trading values.

- Use Idea Sheet 6–10 to write your ideas of what would make a penny magical.
- Evaluate the advantages and disadvantages of a magic penny. List your ideas on different sides of a penny shape. Add this to the writing from the activity above to make a penny booklet.

Social Studies Teaching Activities
Skill: Self-Concept

- Make a poster of yourself surrounded by the people who love you.
- In a mobile, show the different loving actions of someone who loves you. See the example at right.
- Create "loving care coupons" using Idea Sheet 6–11. Write different good deeds you could do to help scmeone you love on each coupon. Deliver the coupons.
- Make some personal observations. When you give away a loving care coupon, notice the person's reaction. Give yourself a pat on the back for a job well done!

Science Teaching Activities
Skill: Changes

- The song "Magic Penny" shows love given away and then returned as a lot more. What living things and nonliving things also multiply? Show them in an illustrated sequence.

- Start an edible experiment! Use "Grandma's Friendship Cake" to show how yeast multiplies the beginning amount of cake batter.

Grandma's Friendship Cake

Starter: 1 package active dry yeast
2 cups lukewarm water
2 cups flour

Dissolve the yeast in the lukewarm water in a large glass bowl. Add flour and beat until smooth. Cover and let rise at room temperature for 48 hours.

To begin the cake mix:

Day 1— Divide the starter batter into large bowls, 1 cup per bowl. Stir, cover, and set on counter. Do not refrigerate!

Days 2, 3, and 4— Stir batter, cover, and return to counter.

Day 5— Add 1 cup milk, 1 cup flour, and 1 cup sugar. Stir well, cover, and return to counter.

Days 6, 7, and 8— Stir, cover, and return to counter.

Day 9— Add 1 cup milk, 1 cup flour, and 1 cup sugar. Stir well. Remove 3 cups of batter and give to 3 friends with a copy of this recipe.

To the remaining batter, add ⅔ cup oil, 3 cups sugar, 2 cups flour, 1½ tsp. cinnamon, ½ tsp. salt, 2 tsp. baking powder, and ½ tsp. baking soda. Mix well and add 2 tsp. vanilla. Beat until smooth.

Then fold in *any* combinations of nuts, dried fruits, chopped apples, grated carrots, mashed bananas, etc.

Bake in a greased tube or loaf pan for 55–60 minutes in a 350° F oven.

- Consider the words "hold it tight and you won't have any." What could happen to interrupt the growth of the sequences illustrated in the first activity? Show your ideas in a flip-up picture.

- Using Idea Sheet 6–12, draw a set of pictures of something you'd like to see multiply.
- Evaluate the things classmates wish would multiply. Which are a real possibility and which are an imaginary possibility? Why? Write a brief explanation on a note to post next to each idea.

Magic Penny

Name ______________________

IDEA SHEET 6–9

Directions: List ways your family, friends, acquaintances, and distant relatives show they care about you. Compare them with each other. What similarities and differences are there?

CARE GIVER	ACTION	COMPARISON
Dad	tucks me in bed and reads to me	Grandma always reads to me, too!

BONUS! On the back of this sheet, list ways *you* show care for your family, friends, acquaintances, and distant relatives.

Magic Penny

Name ____________________

IDEA SHEET 6–10

Directions: What would make a penny magical? Tell about it!

Magic Penny

Name ____________________

IDEA SHEET 6–11

Directions: On each loving care coupon, list good deeds you could do to help a particular friend or relative. Cut out the coupons and deliver them.

Loving Care Coupon To: For: ________ Signed	Loving Care Coupon To: For: ________ Signed
Loving Care Coupon To: For: ________ Signed	Loving Care Coupon To: For: ________ Signed

© 1992 by The Center for Applied Research in Education

Name ______________________

IDEA SHEET 6–12

Directions: Think of something you'd like to see magically multiplied. Draw and tell about it in the space below.

© 1992 by The Center for Applied Research in Education

OPEN-ENDED IDEA SHEET

© 1992 by The Center for Applied Research in Education

7

March

SYLVESTER AND THE MAGIC PEBBLE
Written and Illustrated by William Steig

(New York: Simon & Schuster, 1969)

Caldecott Medal Winner, 1970

Sylvester Duncan, a donkey who lives with his mother and father in a rural community, enjoys collecting pebbles. One day he finds a magic pebble. As he is walking home imagining all the things he might wish for, he innocently turns himself into a rock to escape a ferocious lion. The story follows the family's feelings as a year passes. Then a May picnic resolves their separation, and the family realizes their most important wish is to have one another always.

Language Arts Teaching Activities
Skill: Story Elements

- Make vocabulary cards of interesting words from the story. Use them in an oral sentence game. Post words on a large pebble shape and let children take turns being Sylvester. Make a Sylvester face mask and encourage each child to choose a word to use in a sentence while holding the mask. As a further challenge, have children use as many words as possible in one sentence. Vocabulary words include

gratified	eventually
fetlock	exclamations

startled	aimlessly
confused	stone-dumb
perplexed	miserable
puzzled	nook
bewildered	gully
ceased	dreadful
pebble	concluded
flaming red	panic
remarkable	helpless
vanished	hopeless
existed	inquiring

- Use Idea Sheet 7–1 to make donkey silhouettes on which to list characteristics of Mr. and Mrs. Duncan and Sylvester. Compare each profile to friends and family. Who do you know who shares some of the attributes?
- Have each child bring a pebble to school and then take an imaginary "pebble walk." Where would their pebbles take them? What would they see, hear, smell, touch, and perhaps taste? Write ideas in a guided imagery form. Take time to share.
- Chart the emotions of the story from the different characters' viewpoints. Consider their reactions to the different situations. How do people react to those same situations? What advice could be given to Sylvester (and to others) who might end up in some of the same situations?

Math Teaching Activities
Skill: Sets

- Use Idea Sheet 7–2 to brainstorm all the sets in the story. For example, on page 1 there are sets of donkeys, flowers, furniture, and pebbles. On index cards, draw pictures of sets from the book to use with the next activity.
- Make a game of comparing the index card sets. Have children hold up a set at random. What mathematical statement(s) can they make? Encourage the use of mathematical terms such as *equal, greater than, less than, sum, minuend,* etc.

- Take a second look at the illustrations in the story. Choose one and add an appropriate set to it by re-creating it with chalk or watercolor. Then consider what effect the added set has on the story. In your opinion, if it improves the story, write it on a self-stick note and put it on the corresponding page of the book.

Social Studies Teaching Activities
Skill: Safety, Feelings

- List examples of how we practice behavior (both preventive and emergency) to prepare for crisis situations. Write a safety slogan for one of the situations listed. For example, "Accident Free Classroom!" "Super Safety Students!"
- Compare Sylvester's feelings in the beginning of the book with those at the end. He began thinking of "anything" he could wish for, but he ended up with "all they really wanted." Outline the major factors leading to this change on an accordion fold display.

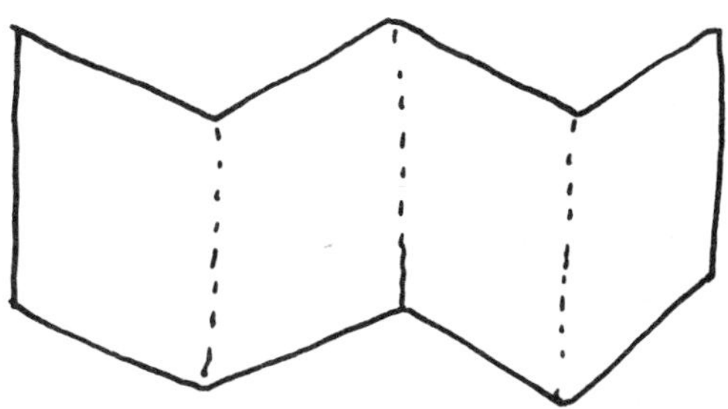

- Think about how Sylvester's actions innocently got him in trouble. On Idea Sheet 7–3, write an advice letter telling Sylvester what to do next time.
- Sylvester ran into difficulty because of the awesome responsibility of a magic pebble. New items can also bring special responsibilities to people (for example, swimming pools, sports equipment, new furniture, heirlooms, etc.). Have students draw these types of things on a cube. Then toss the cube and suggest responsibilities to consider for the item on top of the cube.

Science Teaching Activities
Skill: Seasons

- List all the science-related elements in the story. Consider both weather and nature!
- Depict the story in a seasonal timeline. Make the timeline a moveable strip. If Sylvester had found the pebble in a different season, how would the story change?

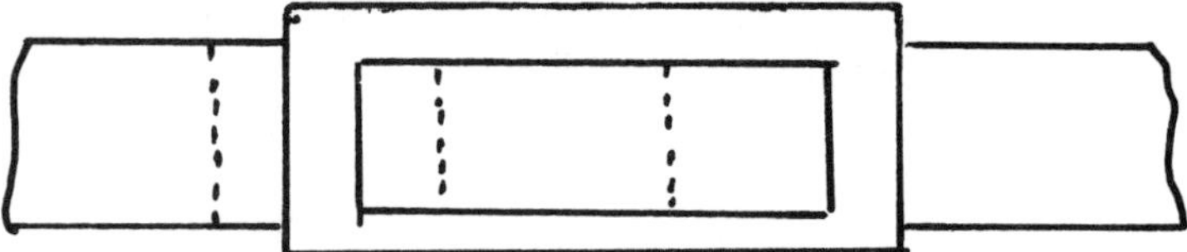

- Combine the different settings of the story in an environmental mural. Add scientific labels.
- A humorous element of the book is that Sylvester is in an incongruous setting. What would happen if the story were in a different environment (for example, outer space, desert, or rain forest)? Would Sylvester still find a magic pebble? What weather and nature elements would change? Use Idea Sheet 7-4 to organize your thinking and predict how the setting change would affect the story.

Name ______________________

SYLVESTER AND THE MAGIC PEBBLE *IDEA SHEET 7–1*

Directions: Choose one of the donkey characters of the book. List all the characteristics that are mentioned and implied in the story.

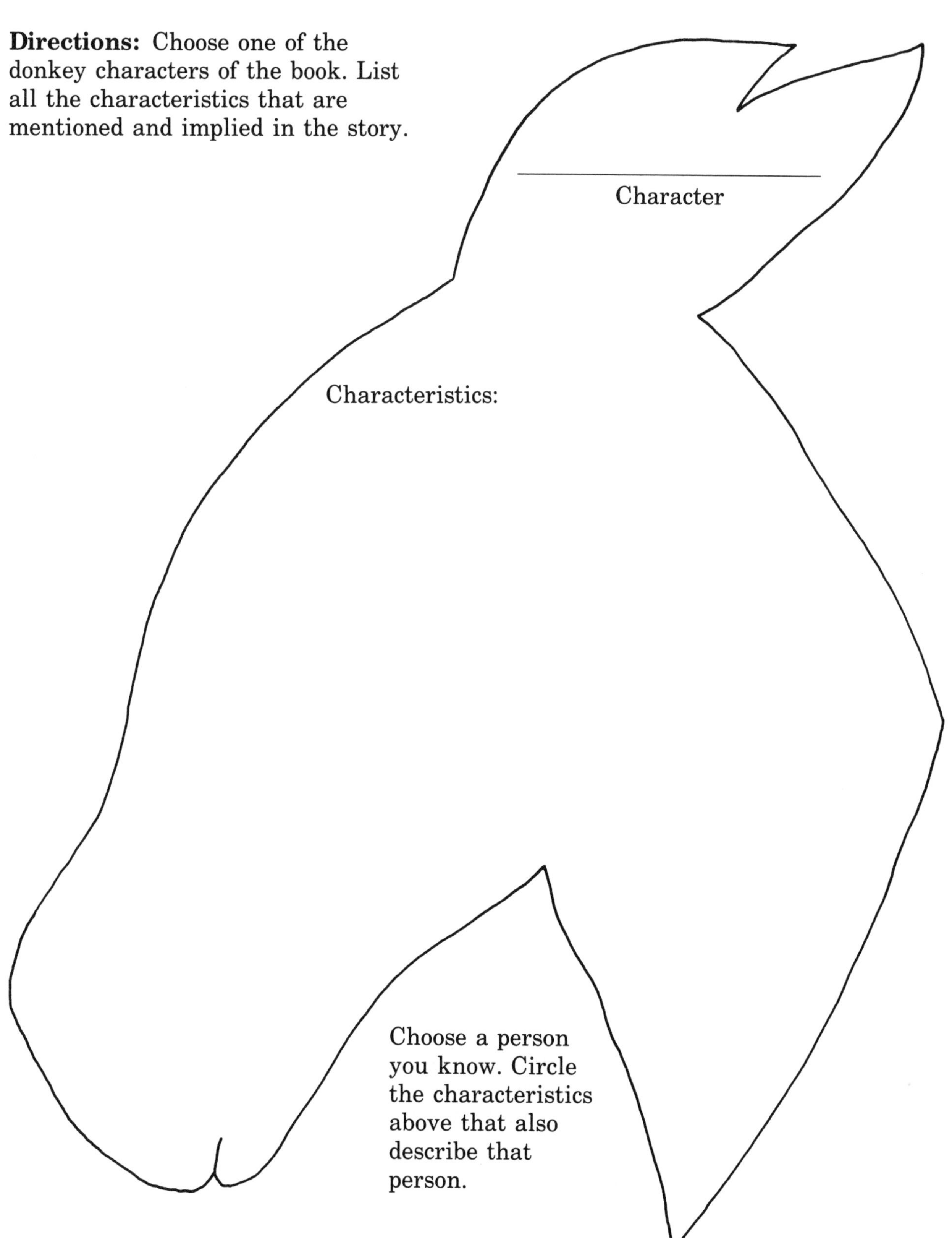

© 1992 by The Center for Applied Research in Education

Name ____________________________

SYLVESTER AND THE MAGIC PEBBLE *IDEA SHEET 7–2*

Directions: On the donkey shape, make a long list of all the sets contained in the story.

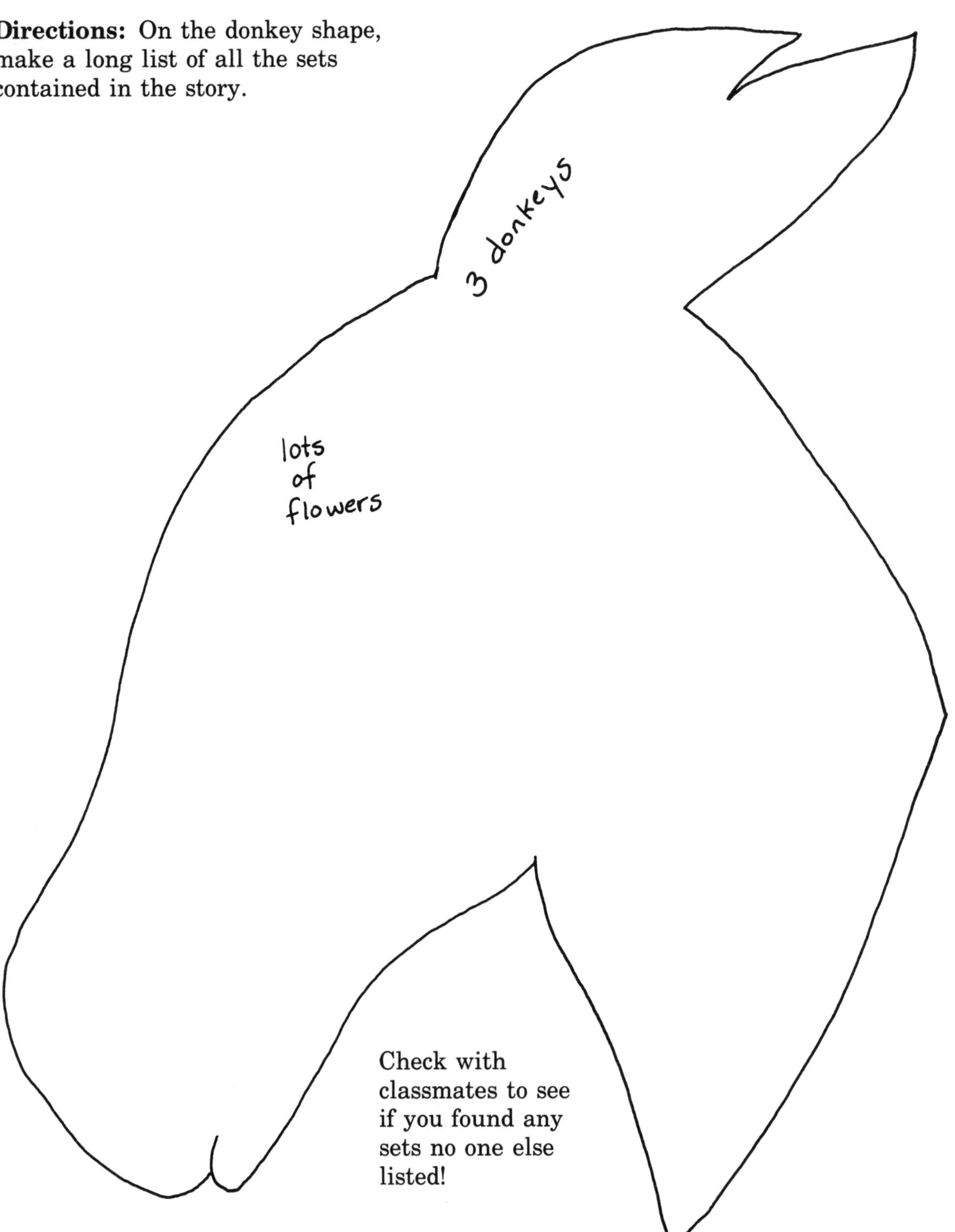

Check with classmates to see if you found any sets no one else listed!

© 1992 by The Center for Applied Research in Education

Name ______________________________

SYLVESTER AND THE MAGIC PEBBLE *IDEA SHEET 7–3*

Directions: Write a letter to Sylvester. Give him suggestions and advice for how to avoid the same problem or how to solve the same problem should he find himself in trouble again.

Dear Sylvester,

© 1992 by The Center for Applied Research in Education

Name ______________________________

SYLVESTER AND THE MAGIC PEBBLE *IDEA SHEET 7–4*

Directions: On the donkey shape, list all the story settings you can think of. Choose one of the settings you listed. On the back of this sheet, write how the new setting would affect the story as written by William Steig.

© 1992 by The Center for Applied Research in Education

Name ______________________________

SYLVESTER AND THE MAGIC PEBBLE

OPEN-ENDED IDEA SHEET

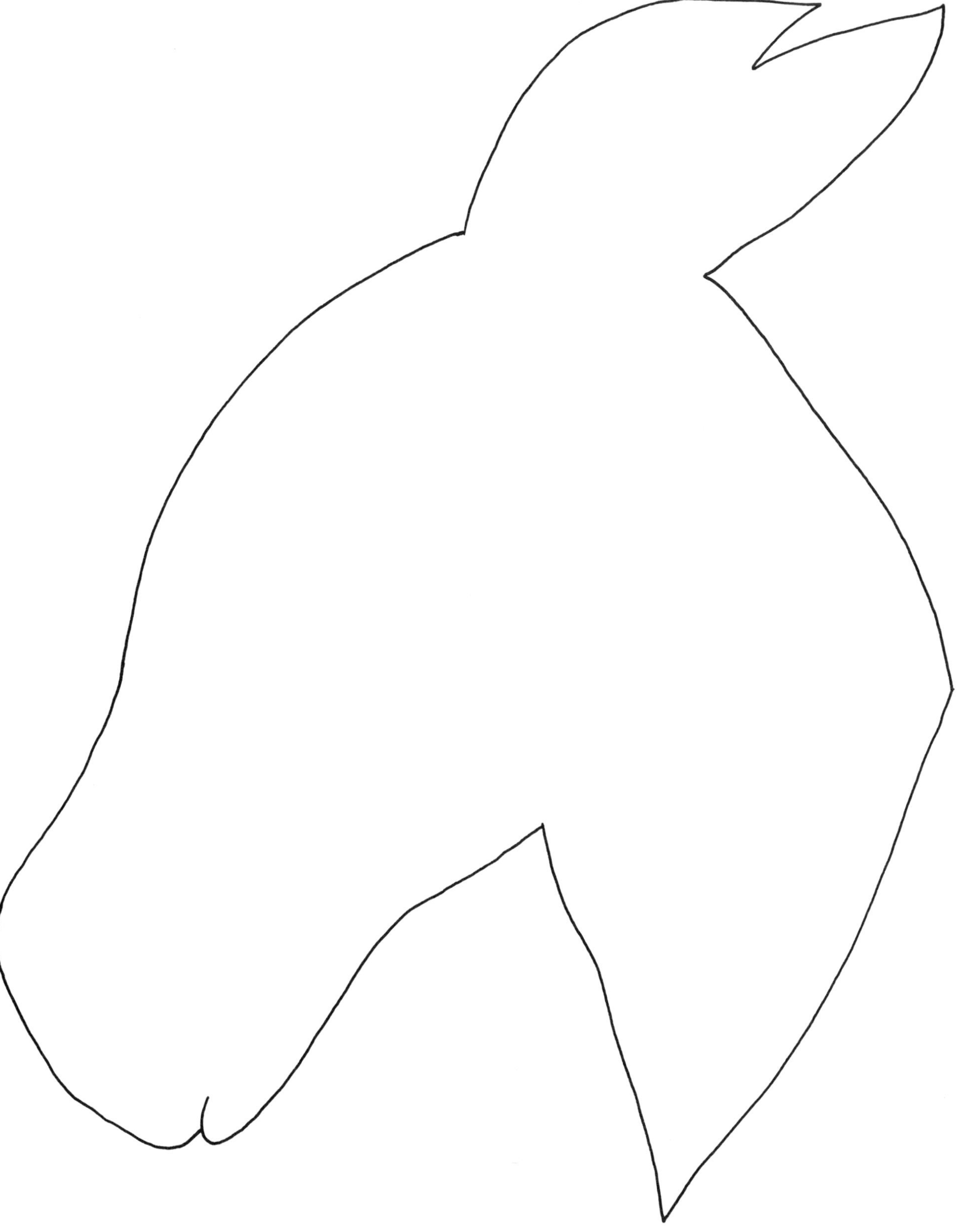

© 1992 by The Center for Applied Research in Education

"Windy Words"
by Jean Conder Soule

I am the Wind
And you'd better watch out!
I can run, I can fly;
I can whistle and shout.

I can tap on your window
And howl at your door,
Tug on your coat tails,
Bellow and roar.

But in March I'm the loudest;
Look out for my might!
For when you're not looking
I'll steal your new kite.

MY ILLUSTRATION

© 1992 by The Center for Applied Research in Education

"WINDY WORDS"
by Jean Conder Soule
from Poetry Place Anthology

(New York: Instructor Books, 1983)

Language Arts Teaching Activities
Skill: Vocabulary

- Use a thesaurus to add to the words describing the wind: *flutter, gust,* etc. Record the words on Idea Sheet 7-5.
- Categorize the windy words on Idea Sheet 7-5 according to spring, summer, fall, and winter winds. Create a seasonal booklet of the words.
- Compose further verses to the poem and illustrate them. For example,

> In April I roar as the storm clouds show,
> When May comes I'm gentle–
> to watch the flowers grow.

- Write an advertisement for your favorite windy word. Clip it on a classroom clothesline.

Math Teaching Activities
Skill: Measurement

- On Idea Sheet 7-6, order the different kinds of wind according to intensity.
- Set up a wind gauge, wind sock, weather vane, and flag that can be seen easily from the classroom window. Gather information about the strength and direction of the wind. Compare information from the different instruments.

- Write a story in which wind gusts get stronger and stronger or weaker and weaker.
- Form committees to evaluate the windy stories written in the activity above. Recommend an award for each story. Awards may include the funniest, most detailed, most scientific, best illustrated, most interesting setting, and so on.

Social Studies Teaching Activities
Skill: Self

- Focus on yourself! Become the wind through creative dramatics.
- Use the Venn diagram on Idea Sheet 7–7 to compare yourself to the wind. What do you have in common? What's different?

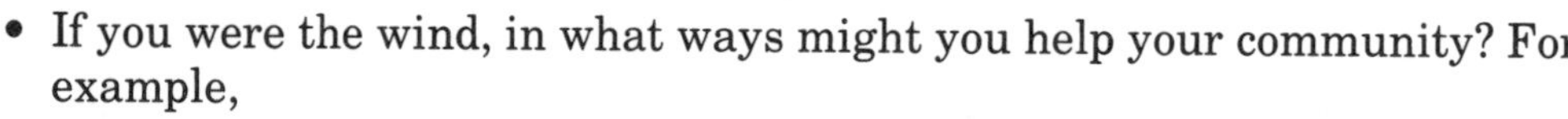

- Write a poem about yourself as if you were the wind.
- If you were the wind, in what ways might you help your community? For example,

  "I'd blow all day for a kite-flying contest."
  "I'd push at marathon runners' backs to help them along."

Science Teaching Activities
Skill: Wind

- Name and illustrate examples of all the different intensities of wind. Use Idea Sheet 7–6 as a reference.
- Research the different types of wind, and write facts on the backs of the illustrations from the previous activity.
- Create wind toys. Make parachutes from various materials; put together a bubbles mixture; construct whirligigs, pinwheels, kites, or wind socks.
- Use Idea Sheet 7–8 to report on the ways people put wind power to use. Consider both work-related and decorative uses. What conclusions can be made about the value of wind power?

Windy Words

Name ______________________

IDEA SHEET 7–5

Directions: Use a thesaurus to list words that name or describe wind. Check the seasons to which they apply.

WORDS	SPRING	SUMMER	FALL	WINTER
flutter	✓	✓		

Circle the words that are new for you. Try to use them in your writings or conversations soon!

© 1992 by The Center for Applied Research in Education

Windy Words

Name ______________________________

IDEA SHEET 7–6

Directions: Research all the different kinds of windy conditions (zephyr, hurricane, etc.). Briefly describe them below. Then put them in order according to intensity.

zephyr - the west wind, any soft gentle breeze

Windy Words

Name ______________________________

IDEA SHEET 7–7

Directions: Compare yourself to the wind on the Venn diagram below.

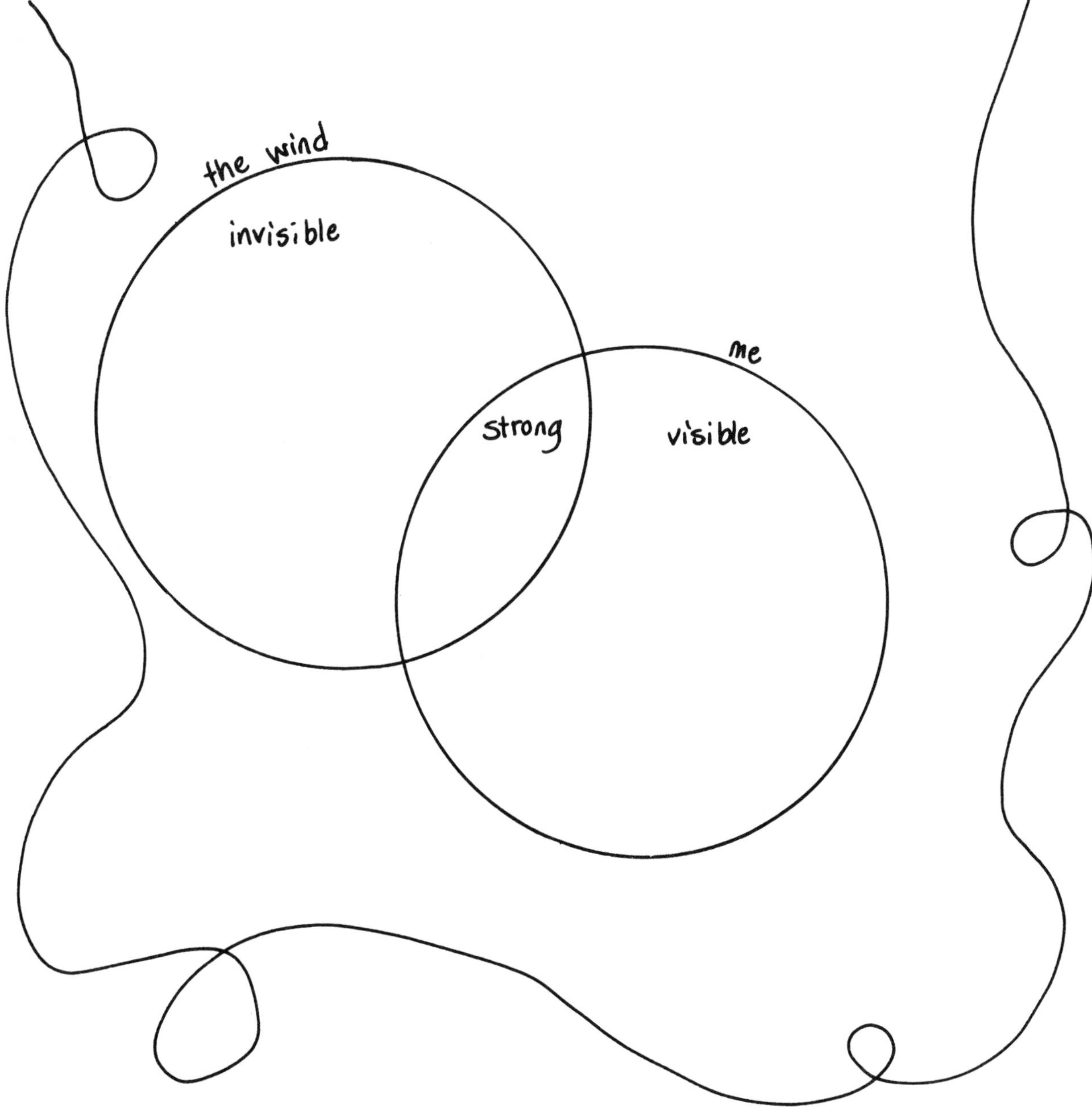

Windy Words

Name ______________________________

IDEA SHEET 7–8

Directions: Make a long list of ways people use wind power. Ask other people if they can add ideas to your list.

What conclusions can you draw about the value of wind power?

© 1992 by The Center for Applied Research in Education

Windy Words

OPEN-ENDED IDEA SHEET

© 1992 by The Center for Applied Research in Education

"Down by the Bay"
(Traditional Song)

Down by the bay, where the watermelons grow,
Back to my home, I dare not go,
For if I do, my mother will say . . .
Did you ever see a goose, kissing a moose,
Down by the bay?

Down by the bay, where the watermelons grow,
Back to my home, I dare not go,
For if I do, my mother will say . . .
Did you ever see a whale, with a polka dot tail,
Down by the bay?

Down by the bay, where the watermelons grow,
Back to my home, I dare not go,
For if I do, my mother will say . . .
Did you ever see a fly, wearing a tie,
Down by the bay?

Down by the bay, where the watermelons grow,
Back to my home, I dare not go,
For if I do, my mother will say . . .
Did you ever see a bear, combing his hair,
Down by the bay?

Down by the bay, where the watermelons grow,
Back to my home, I dare not go,
For if I do, my mother will say . . .
Did you ever see llamas, eating their pajamas,
Down by the bay?

Down by the bay, where the watermelons grow,
Back to my home, I dare not go,
For if I do, my mother will say . . .
Did you ever have a time, when you couldn't make a rhyme,
Down by the bay? Down by the bay?

MY ILLUSTRATION

© 1992 by The Center for Applied Research in Education

"Down by the Bay"
Traditional Song

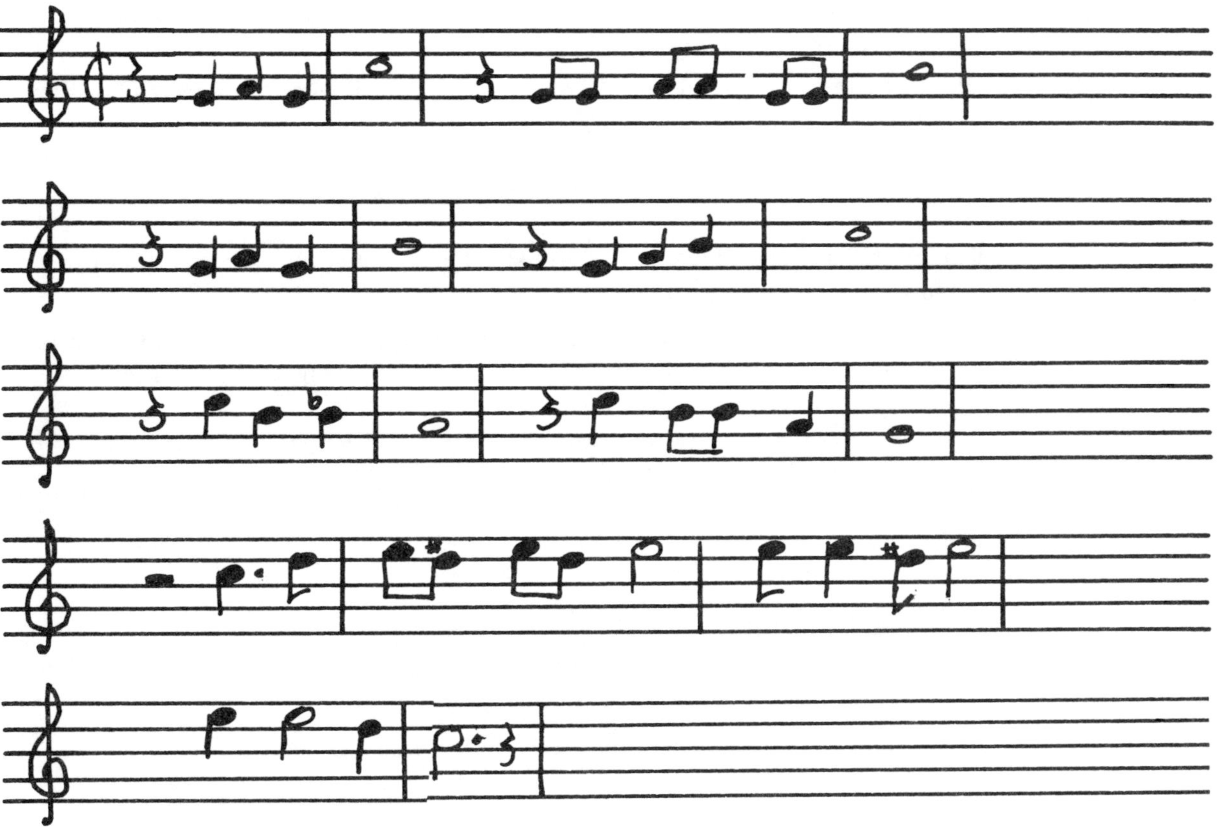

© 1992 by The Center for Applied Research in Education

"DOWN BY THE BAY"
(Traditional Song)

Language Arts Teaching Activities
Skill: Nonsense Verse

- Ask students to bring from home examples of this song. Check the library for different versions, too. Use Idea Sheet 7–9 to compare two different versions of the song.

- Identify the nonsense elements in the song and illustrate the phrases. For example,

  a goose kissing a moose

  Consider what would happen if you saw these nonsense things happening! Choose one and list all the consequences.
- What nonsense verses can you add to the song? Start by listing rhyming words. Make a silly combination. For example with *dove* and *glove,*

  Did you ever see a dove, stitching a glove,
  Down by the bay?

- Rate the new verses for their nonsense value. List the consequences each verse would have, and see what category your verse fits:

  0–5 consequences = Whoopido!

  5–10 consequences = Zowie-wowie!

  10 or more consequences = Fantastico!

  Encourage children to design their own nonsense awards.

Math Teaching Activities
Skill: Problem Solving

- Use Idea Sheet 7–10 to write word problems to go with each stanza. Compile them in an illustrated class book. For example,

  If three geese were kissing three moose,
  how many animals would be in the verse?

- Check the skills involved for the word problems in the class book. Compare them with the expected grade level skills. Generate problems for the skills that have not been covered.

- Add numbers to the verses. For example,

  Did you ever see a two, on your Daddy's shoe,
  Down by the bay?

- Illustrate the verses from the preceding activity. Teach them to a younger child using the picture and showing the number. Then check to see if the child can find the number on a number line. Did the song seem to help teach a number? Why or why not?

Social Studies Teaching Activities
Skill: Geography

- Use a map to identify lots of water terms: *bay, stream, inlet,* etc. Create a make-believe map that shows all the different types of water areas.
- Compare students' maps. What differences can be noted? similarities? Write observations on an experience chart.
- Change the song to include different types of water areas on Idea Sheet 7–11.
- Evaluate the original song and the new verses according to the geography of your area. Is there a bay, stream, inlet, etc. nearby? Give examples.

Science Teaching Activities
Skill: Animals

- Cut out shapes of the animals in the song. Record facts about the animals on their shapes.
- Use Idea Sheet 7–12 to list lots of different animals. Then list lots of words that rhyme with each animal. Change the song to incorporate facts about the animals and appropriate rhyming words. Or create verses for new animals!
- Share the new factual version of the song and the traditional version of the song with other students. Survey to discover which is more popular. Chart student responses to support your answer.

Name ______________________

DOWN BY THE BAY

IDEA SHEET 7–9

Directions: Share two versions of the song with friends and family. Survey to find the more popular version.

	Version 1	Version 2
Votes (tally marks)		
reasons why		

© 1992 by The Center for Applied Research in Education

Name ______________________

DOWN BY THE BAY

IDEA SHEET 7–10

Directions: List three math skills you have studied this year. Using ideas from the song, write a word problem that provides practice for each skill.

math skills	word problems

© 1992 by The Center for Applied Research in Education

Name ______________________

DOWN BY THE BAY

IDEA SHEET 7–11

Directions: Make a long list of geographical features that include water.

Choose one of the water features to modify the song.

© 1992 by The Center for Applied Research in Education

Name ______________________________

DOWN BY THE BAY

IDEA SHEET 7–12

Directions: List lots of animals. Beside each animal, list some words that rhyme. Or list words you'll want to use in a new verse of the song, and try to think of an animal that rhymes with those words. For example, *dove: glove, love, above.*

© 1992 by The Center for Applied Research in Education

Now create new verses for the song using silly combinations from your list. For example,

Did you ever see a dove, stitching a glove,
Down by the bay?

DOWN BY THE BAY

OPEN-ENDED IDEA SHEET

© 1992 by The Center for Applied Research in Education

8

April

A TREE IS NICE
by Janice Mary Udry
Illustrated by Marc Simont
(New York: Harper and Row, 1956)
Caldecott Medal Winner, 1957

In this book, the author phrases simple yet encompassing descriptions of how people use and enjoy trees. The text and illustrations encourage readers to consider personal situations where they, too, might have thought about the many contributions trees make to our world.

Language Arts Teaching Activities
Skill: Literature about Trees

- Collect other poems and stories about trees. List them in an Arbor Day bibliography.
- Begin a display of texture rubbings from tree trunks, branches, and leaves. Compare and contrast them. Encourage children to bring more from home, and add them in the appropriate category.
- Compose individual or class poems and stories about trees. Try beginning with "A tree is nice. . . ." Use Idea Sheet 8–1 to get your thinking started. Consider putting the ideas together into an Arbor Day program.

- Choose a favorite book from the bibliography. Give a book talk encouraging others to read the selection. Videotape the class's book talks to send home for families to enjoy.

Math Teaching Activities
Skill: Collecting and Using Data

- Invite a guest speaker to talk about trees and careers associated with trees. What types of mathematics are involved in planting a tree? Consider proximity to other things, estimating growth, and measurement.
- Compare information about trees from a nursery, mail-order catalog, and forestry department. Use a chart listing types of trees, where they grow well, prices, and any other significant details.
- Use Idea Sheet 8–2 as a log to detail mathematical information about trees. Keep a special log for a tree on the school grounds during the school year. Consider sharing the log idea with park rangers, scouting organizations, or nature groups.

- What facts do you think people don't know about trees? Incorporate them into math word problems about trees. Display the problems on a tree bulletin board and invite another class to solve them. Which problem was missed the most? Why?

Social Studies Teaching Activities
Skill: Communities

- Marc Simont's illustrations depict countryside tree settings. Choose one of his illustrations and show how it would change if the location was a city or a suburb.
- On Idea Sheet 8–3, list how people and trees are interdependent using examples from the story. Display this information on paper chain links.
- Consider the viewpoint of a tree. What would be a tree's response to this book? Choral read the story, interjecting the tree's lines.
- How are trees shown to be important in this book? What criteria can you add to this author's idea list? Prioritize the ideas and illustrate them on a roller movie. (See page 220).

Science Teaching Activities
Skill: Trees

- Use reference books to cut silhouettes of different kinds of trees. Show branch patterns with chalk. Display silhouettes in the windows or hang them from the ceiling.

- In what ways does the environment affect trees? Why do different types of trees grow in particular environments? Use the illustrations in the book to find examples. What other examples can you add? Illustrate your findings.

- Survey the illustrations in the book to determine the needs of a tree. Use Idea Sheet 8–4 to devise an invention to meet one of those needs.
- Organize a "tree report." Using the criteria of soil type, light, proximity to other things, and drainage, evaluate how the trees on your school grounds were planted. What recommendations might be made for future plantings?

Name ______________________________

A TREE IS NICE

IDEA SHEET 8–1

Directions: List all the ways "a tree is nice." Use the ideas you list to compose your own story or poem.

A TREE IS NICE . . .

FOR ANIMALS

FOR PEOPLE

FOR THE EARTH

FOR OTHER REASONS

© 1992 by The Center for Applied Research in Education

Name ______________________

A TREE IS NICE

IDEA SHEET 8–2

Directions: Check lots of resources for mathematical facts about trees. Record the information on this log.

DATE	FACTS	SOURCE	MATHEMATICAL CONCEPT/SKILLS
4-4-93	Redwoods are the largest trees in America. They can reach over 360 ft. tall!	Encyclopedia	measuring height

Compare your log with a friend's log. What observations can you make?

In what ways could the facts you have collected be useful?

© 1992 by The Center for Applied Research in Education

Name ______________________

A TREE IS NICE

IDEA SHEET 8–3

Directions: Make a long list of reasons people find trees useful or necessary.

Make a long list of reasons why trees might need people.

Circle the reasons that are, in your opinion, *very* important.

© 1992 by The Center for Applied Research in Education

Name ______________________

A TREE IS NICE

IDEA SHEET 8–4

Directions: List lots of problems trees can have.

On the back of this sheet, describe and diagram an invention to solve one of the problems you listed.

© 1992 by The Center for Applied Research in Education

A TREE IS NICE

OPEN-ENDED IDEA SHEET

© 1992 by The Center for Applied Research in Education

"Spring Zing"
by Minnie Mondschein

rustling . . .
  rippling . . .
    flutter,
      flap;

bubbling . . .
  billowing . . .
    crackle,
      crack;

stirring . . .
  whirring . . .
    slither,
      snap;

blowing . . .
  flowing . . .
    tinkle,
      tap;

rolling . . .
  tolling . . .
    rip,
      rap;

singing . . .
  ringing . . .
    zip,
      zap.

MY ILLUSTRATION

© 1992 by The Center for Applied Research in Education

"SPRING ZING"
by Minnie Mondschein
from Poetry Place Anthology
(New York: Instructor Books, 1983)

Language Arts Teaching Activities
Skill: Vocabulary

- Use Idea Sheet 8–5 to list nouns to go with all the verbs in the poem.
- Put the nouns and verbs in a flip book. How many are interchangeable?
- Write and illustrate your own version of a Spring Zing poem.
- Evaluate which of the words in "Spring Zing" apply to the spring weather your area experiences.

Math Teaching Activities
Skill: Patterns

- Cut the six circles (one for each stanza) on Idea Sheet 8–6 into fourths. List one word from the poem on each fourth. Pile the fourths together and have students draw four fourths from the pile to make a complete circle. When they read the words, what new rhythms are heard?
- Chart the new rhythm patterns from the previous activity and chart the occurrence of each new rhythm pattern. For example,

New phrase	pattern	# of times drawn tally
billowing, tap, flowing, rap	3-1-2-1	III

- Choose a pattern that you like from the preceding activity's chart. Choose words from the poem to fit that pattern, and then perform your verse with sound effects.

- Make a daily list of spring words that describe the weather for one week. Is there a pattern? Are some words used more than others? Which words don't occur often? What conclusions can be drawn about essential spring words? Why?

Social Studies Teaching Activities
Skill: Neighborhood

- Think of your neighborhood as you read the poem. Then complete the following sentence patterns:

  In my neighborhood, rustling can be ______________________________,

  rippling can be ______________________________,

  Keep going using phrases from the poem.

- What occupations in your neighborhood fit the different spring sounds? List them on Idea Sheet 8–7.

- Create a picture map of your neighborhood and show things happening on the map to go with each sound from the poem.
- Evaluate sounds of spring in your neighborhood. What do you hear? What don't you hear? Why? What sounds, if any, would you add? Why?

Science Teaching Activities
Skill: Sound

- List the words from the poem on cards. Have each student draw a card and act out objects that can make that sound.
- Classify the sounds on Idea Sheet 8–8. Are they made by humans, nature, or a combination? What other classifications can you think of?
- Add a science word to each verb in the poem. For example,

  rustling grass
  rippling puddles

- Collect pictures to make a collage that illustrates the new poem.
- What aspects of spring do *not* go with these sound words? Why? Write them on the back of your collage.

Name ______________________

SPRING ZING

IDEA SHEET 8–5

Directions: Choose verbs from the poem. List lots of nouns to go with each verb.

VERB	NOUNS
example: rustling	leaves, papers, nylon jackets...

Compare your list with friends' lists. Underline the nouns that are duplicated. Circle the nouns no one else thought of.

© 1992 by The Center for Applied Research in Education

Name ______________________

SPRING ZING

IDEA SHEET 8–6

Directions: Rearrange the poem. Cut each circle (stanza) into fourths. Put all of the fourths upside-down in a pile. Draw four fourths and create a new stanza for "Spring Zing."

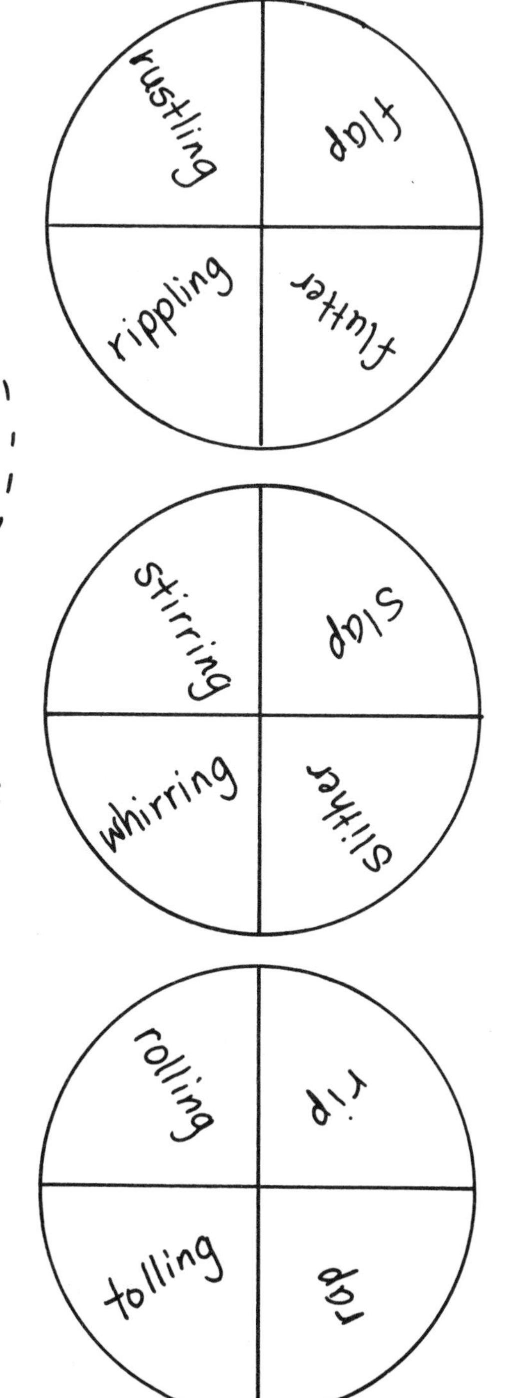

billowing
slap
bubbling
slither

blowing
tap
flowing
tinkle

singing
zip
ringing
zap

© 1992 by The Center for Applied Research in Education

Name ______________________

SPRING ZING

IDEA SHEET 8–7

Directions: List workers you might see in your neighborhood who fit the "Spring Zing" sounds.

SOUND/VERB	OCCUPATIONS
rustling	florist, gift shop

© 1992 by The Center for Applied Research in Education

Name ______________________

SPRING ZING

IDEA SHEET 8–8

Directions: Use this chart to classify the sounds from the poem. Give one example of each category, if possible. Can you think of other categories? Use the last two columns to show your ideas.

SPRING SOUND	HUMAN-MADE	MADE BY NATURE	COMBI-NATION	______	______
rustling	clothing	animal in a tree	walking through grass		

© 1992 by The Center for Applied Research in Education

SPRING ZING

OPEN-ENDED IDEA SHEET

© 1992 by The Center for Applied Research in Education

"Apples and Bananas"
(Traditional Song)

I like to eat, eat, eat,
Apples and bananas;
I like to eat, eat, eat,
Apples and bananas.

I like to ate, ate, ate,
Ape-puls and ba-nay-nays;
I like to ate, ate, ate,
Ape-puls and ba-nay-nays.

I like to eat, eat, eat,
Ee-puls and bee-nee-nees;
I like to eat, eat, eat,
Ee-puls and bee-nee-nees.

I like to ite, ite, ite
I-puls and bi-ni-nis;
I like to ite, ite, ite
I-puls and bi-ni-nis.

I like to oat, oat, oat,
O-puls and bo-no-nos;
I like to oat, oat, oat,
O-puls and bo-no-nos.

I like to oot, oot, oot,
Oo-puls and boo-noo-noos;
I like to oot, oot, oot,
Oo-puls and boo-noo-noos;

Repeat first verse.

MY ILLUSTRATION

© 1992 by The Center for Applied Research in Education

"Apples and Bananas"
Traditional Song

© 1992 by The Center for Applied Research in Education

"APPLES AND BANANAS"
(Traditional Song)

Language Arts Teaching Activities
Skill: Long Vowels

- Make a poster for each long vowel sound illustrating the corresponding verse.
- When the long vowel sound is substituted in verses two through six, which words become nonsense and which are still "real" words? Tally and draw conclusions on Idea Sheet 8–9.
- Compose silly definitions for the words that change to nonsense.
- Survey friends and family members to evaluate the use of repetition in the song. Support whether it's a positive or negative part of the song.

Survey

What's your opinion of the repetition in the song "Apples and Bananas?"

Person	Positive- liked it (plus reason)	Negative- didn't like it (plus reason)	No opinion
Mom	X - because it's fun!		

Math Teaching Activities
Skill: Measurement

- Ask students to bring apples and bananas to school. Record measurements using Idea Sheet 8–10 and a class record chart.
- How many different ways can the apples and bananas be sorted? Keep a list of the attributes used to distinguish different sets.
- Use paper cut in apple and banana shapes to create an imaginary character.

- Consider measurement facts of the cut-paper apple and banana figures. How tall are they? How long are the arms? legs? bodies? How many extra details does each have? Choose the most unusual figures and math facts for a class record book.

Social Studies Teaching Activities
Skill: Folk Crafts

- Invite a craft artist to discuss his or her work with the class. Collect craft magazines and idea books for a classroom display.
- Research important things to consider when working with apples and bananas. For example, bananas quickly turn brown once cut. Record information on Idea Sheet 8–11. Make recommendations for working with apples and bananas as a craft medium.
- Choose an apple or banana craft project to try.

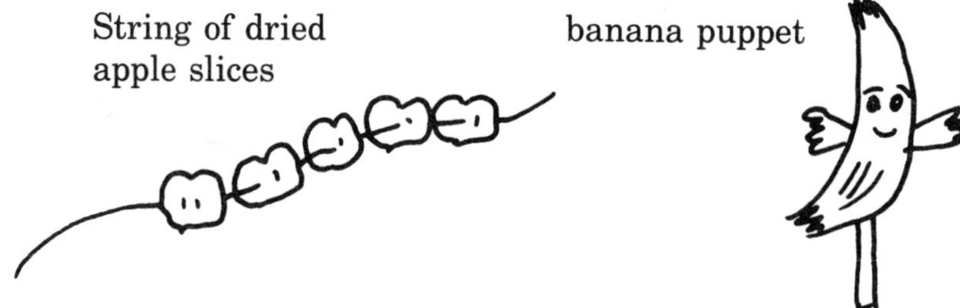

- Write your opinion of craft work. Do you enjoy it? Why or why not? Students who enjoy craft work may be interested in forming a crafters club.

Science Teaching Activities
Skill: Nutrition

- Apples and Bananas begins an alphabetical listing of fruits. Continue the list on Idea Sheet 8–12. Collect or draw pictures of each fruit for an alphabet book.
- Use fruit growers' brochures and the library to collect nutrition information about apples and bananas. Write the information on the front of a 4″ × 6″ index card and illustrate the fruit on the opposite side. Create a display of your research project for your school library.
- Make a friendship salad with the whole class. Each student brings in a piece of fruit, which the teacher cuts up and combines in a large bowl. (A

bonus activity at the analysis level of thinking would be to graph the kinds of fruit that are contributed.)

- Make apple and banana advertisements (written or pictorial). Evaluate the information from the apple and banana information index cards (see activity above) to include information that would convince people of the importance of apples and bananas.

Name ____________________

APPLES AND BANANAS

IDEA SHEET 8–9

Directions: Complete the chart for each of the modified words from the song.

	REAL WORD	NON-SENSE WORD	SOUNDS LIKE ______
ate	X		
ape-puls		X	sounds like apples
ba-nay-nays			
eat			
ee-puls			
bee-nee-nees			
ite			
eye-puls			
bi-ni-nis			
oat			
o-puls			
bo-no-nos			
oot			
oo-puls			
boo-noo-noos			

Compose silly definitions for some of the nonsense words.

Example: Ape-pulls are pull toys invented to entertain zoo animals!

© 1992 by The Center for Applied Research in Education

Name ______________________

APPLES AND BANANAS

IDEA SHEET 8–10

Directions: Use this chart to record measurements of real apples and bananas.

FRUIT	HEIGHT	WEIGHT	CIRCUM-FERENCE	OTHER: ______
Apple 1				
2				
3				
4				
5				
6				
Banana 1				
2				
3				
4				
5				
6				

© 1992 by The Center for Applied Research in Education

Name ______________________

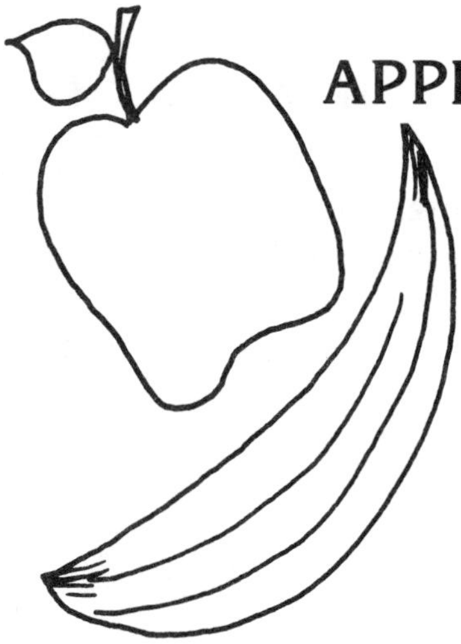

APPLES AND BANANAS

IDEA SHEET 8–11

Directions: Write attributes of each fruit on the appropriate shape.

On the back of this sheet, write conclusions you can draw regarding the use of apples and/or bananas as a craft medium.

© 1992 by The Center for Applied Research in Education

Name ______________________

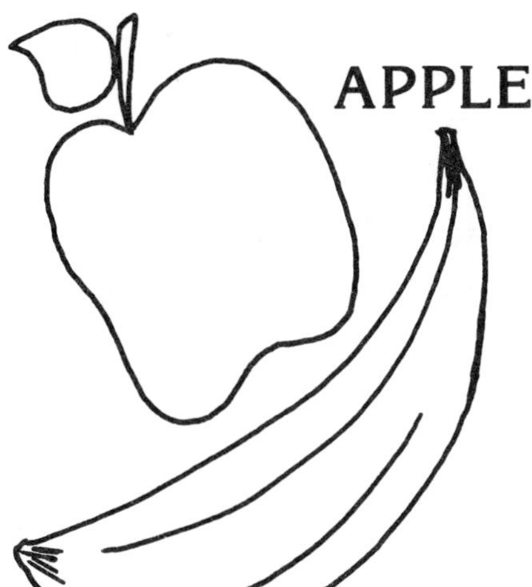

APPLES AND BANANAS

IDEA SHEET 8–12

Directions: Complete the alphabetical listing of fruits. More than one fruit can be written for any letter of the alphabet.

A - apples

B - bananas

C

D

E

F

G

H

I

J

K

L

M

N

O

P

Q

R

S

T

U

V

W

X

Y

Z

© 1992 by The Center for Applied Research in Education

APPLES AND BANANAS

OPEN-ENDED IDEA SHEET

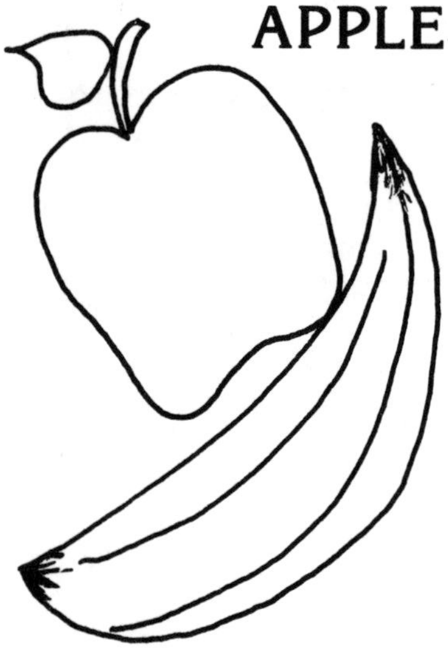

© 1992 by The Center for Applied Research in Education

9

May

THE GIRL WHO LOVED WILD HORSES
Written and Illustrated by Paul Goble
(New York: Macmillan, 1978)
Caldecott Medal Winner, 1979

This is the story of an Indian girl who loves and understands wild horses in a special way. She spends every possible minute with the tribe's herd of horses. One day a terrible thunderstorm startles the horses into a stampede; the girl rides off with them and becomes a companion to a wild stallion. Hunters reclaim the lost girl, but she misses the horses and chooses to return to them to run free.

Language Arts Teaching Activities
Skill: Elements of the Book

- Notice how the artist has overlaid objects in the illustrations to create depth. Choose an illustration from the book to re-create using a mixture of art media. Work from the background of the picture forward. Write about what it was like to experiment with this art technique.
- Survey the illustrations for information that supplements the story. Write a paragraph summarizing the additional details.
- Take a second look at the poem and song included at the end of the story. Use Idea Sheet 9–1 to discuss the imagery the writer uses. For example, the fetlock is described as a fine eagle plume. Compose other images that would be appropriate for horses.

- Why do you suppose the author included the song and poem at the end of the story? Defend your opinion.

Math Teaching Activities
Skill: Patterns

- Give each student a 2″ × 2″ square of paper and have him or her copy a pattern from one of the illustrations. Display the small patterns and encourage children to identify which illustrations they match.

- Investigate the use of symmetry, congruence, and similarity in the illustrations. Draw a teaching poster to illustrate one of these concepts using an example from the book.
- Choose one of the patterns from the display described above. Make a pattern strip as long as the door, to stretch the length of the classroom, to post down the hallway, etc.
- Using Idea Sheet 9–2 judge the use of patterns in the illustrations. Where do they enhance the illustration? Where might they be distracting to the viewer's eye? (Use the think-pair-share strategy described on page 15.)

Social Studies Teaching Activities
Skill: American Indians

- Use cut-out tepees from Idea Sheet 9–3 to mark pages in the story that provide information about Plains Indians. Collect other books about Plains Indians and highlight new facts in the same way.

- In a class discussion distinguish modern Indians from historical Indians. Chart the change of traditional and modern dress, occupations, food, or other attributes.
- Use the facts from the preceding activities to create an Indian card game.
- Survey other classes on their knowledge of Indian facts. Which facts are widely known? Which facts are not well-known? Which facts should be shared to help dispel stereotypes?

Science Teaching Activities
Skill: Hooved Animals

- Make a long list of hooved animals on Idea Sheet 9–4. Chart their needs and habits.
- Form committees to research the different varieties of hooved animals.

What behavior patterns do they all share? Display findings on bulletin board drawings of the species.

- Write a story in which the main character forms a strong friendship with a hooved animal. Incorporate facts about the species in the story.
- Verify how this story, *The Girl Who Loved Wild Horses,* shows the Indians' respect for animals. Select evidence in the illustrations and text. In what ways is such respect important?

Name ______________________________

THE GIRL WHO LOVED WILD HORSES *IDEA SHEET 9–1*

Directions: Enjoy imagery! List features of a wild horse. Choose one feature and make comparisons.

The ________ (part)	is like a ________	because ________.
example: The fetlock	is like a plume	because of the way it flounces in the wind.

© 1992 by The Center for Applied Research in Education

Name ______________________

THE GIRL WHO LOVED WILD HORSES *IDEA SHEET 9–2*

Directions: Find three examples of patterns in the illustrations of the book. For each patterning, use a section of the tepee to

1. identify the pattern you chose,
2. write whether you liked it or didn't like it,
3. tell why.

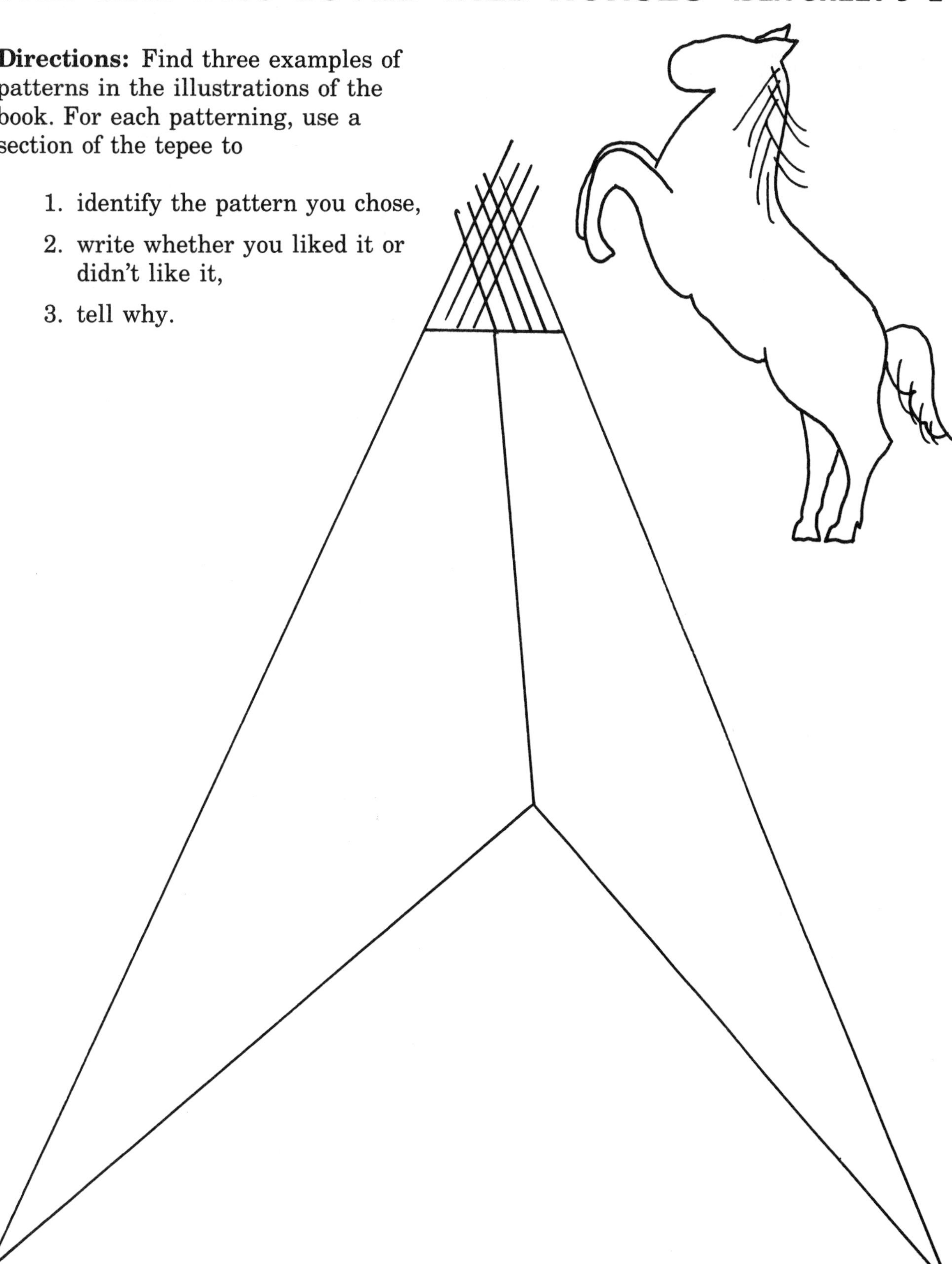

© 1992 by The Center for Applied Research in Education

Name ______________________

THE GIRL WHO LOVED WILD HORSES *IDEA SHEET 9–3*

Directions: The illustrations of the book tell you a lot about the Plains Indians of long ago. Use cut-out tepee shapes to mark pages that provide such information. Write on the tepee bookmarks the information that is either directly provided or that can be inferred.

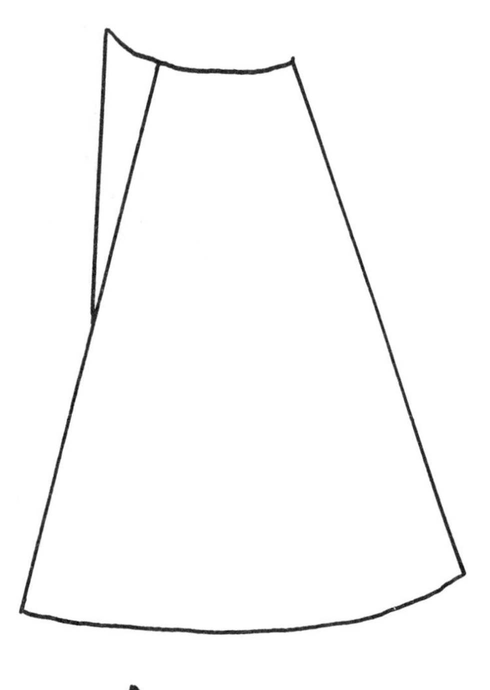

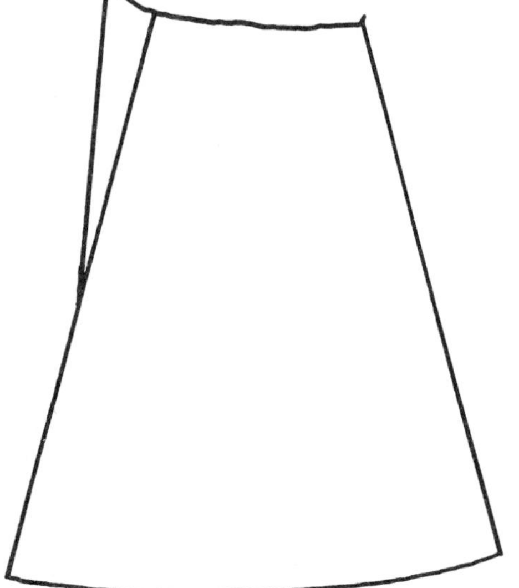

© 1992 by The Center for Applied Research in Education

Name ______________________

THE GIRL WHO LOVED WILD HORSES *IDEA SHEET 9–4*

Directions: Complete the chart to learn about hooved animals. Add other hooved animals and categories that interest you.

Use information from the chart to write a report or a story to share with your class.

HOOVED ANIMAL	WHERE IT LIVES	WHAT IT EATS	WHO ITS ENEMIES ARE	
Cattle	farms, fields, plains	grass, hay	wolves	

© 1992 by The Center for Applied Research in Education

THE GIRL WHO LOVED WILD HORSES

OPEN-ENDED IDEA SHEET

© 1992 by The Center for Applied Research in Education

"Exercises"
by Bette Killion

Stand tall and stretch,
  reach up, up high;
  pretend you're a tree
  growing right through the sky.

Bend to the floor
  with your knees held straight;
  touch your heels 'till you look
  like the figure eight.

Spread out your arms
  from your waist, turn half round;
  back and forth like a clock
  that is being wound.

Hop, hop on one foot;
  then hop on the other;
  pretend you're a bird
  bobbing after its mother.

Leap up so high
  you could jump in a nest
  then flop down, cross-legged,
  and take your rest.

MY ILLUSTRATION

© 1992 by The Center for Applied Research in Education

"EXERCISES"
by Bette Killion
from Poetry Place Anthology
(New York: Instructor Books, 1983)

Language Arts Teaching Activities
Skill: Following Directions

- Follow the directions in the poem. Read them in different sequences for subsequent exercise times.
- What words might you add to the directions to make them easier to follow? Use Idea Sheet 9–5 to record your ideas. Test them on a younger student.
- Add a stanza to the poem that describes another kind of exercise.
- Why would two people follow the same direction differently? Evaluate which directions are very clear and which are open to different interpretations.

Math Teaching Activities
Skill: Measurement

- Add measurement terms to the lines in the poem. For example,

  Stand tall and stretch five extra inches,
  reach up ten centimeters high.

- Compare the measurements you've added to the poem. Illustrate a person doing the exercises in sequence. Use a ruler to make your illustration accurate.
- Consider the tree, figure eight, clock, bird, and nest mentioned in the poem. What could be substituted for those things and still be appropriate for the height of the exercise? Use Idea Sheet 9–6 to organize your ideas. Draw sets of the new ideas, and display them with the poem.
- Time the exercises in the poem. Which take the longest? Which are the quickest? Why?

Social Studies Teaching Activities
Skill: Cooperation Partners

- Enjoy the exercises with a partner.
- Analyze the various exercises. Which are easier done individually? Which are easier done with a partner? Use the chart on Idea Sheet 9–7 to show your thinking.
- Invent a partner exercise. Devise a class partner exercise routine to teach to another class.
- Which exercises would you recommend for someone younger, older, or handicapped in one way? Why?

Science Teaching Activities
Skill: Health

- On Idea Sheet 9–8, make a long list of exercises kids naturally do.
- What else besides exercising is important to maintaining good health? Draw ideas on posters for a school-wide display.
- Create a guide to kids' fitness using information from the two previous activities.
- Create personal health checklists. Evaluate yourself using the checklist. What should you add to your daily routine? Write an editorial about how to get someone else involved in health consciousness.

Name ______________________________

EXERCISES

IDEA SHEET 9–5

Directions: Write complete directions on how to do a favorite exercise. **Hint:** Use a friend to model the exercise for you.

Check your directions by having another friend follow them exactly. Revise your directions, if necessary.

© 1992 by The Center for Applied Research in Education

Name ____________________

EXERCISES

IDEA SHEET 9–6

Directions: Complete the chart by listing items that have the same attributes as the item in the box.

EXAMPLE	
TREE	ATTRIBUTES: Long, tall, thin SIMILAR ITEMS: telephone pole, laundry line, ladder
8	ATTRIBUTES: SIMILAR ITEMS:
CLOCK	ATTRIBUTES: SIMILAR ITEMS:
BIRD	ATTRIBUTES: SIMILAR ITEMS:
NEST	ATTRIBUTES: SIMILAR ITEMS:

Circle the words that make sense when substituted in the poem. Star the word you like best for each verse.

© 1992 by The Center for Applied Research in Education

Name ____________________

EXERCISES

IDEA SHEET 9–7

Directions: Complete the chart to show whether the exercises from the poem are more easily done as an individual or with a partner. Add some other familiar exercises to the chart.

INDI-VIDUAL	PARTNER	EXERCISE
√		stand tall and stretch

Share this chart with your P.E. teacher or coach.

© 1992 by The Center for Applied Research in Education

Name ______________________

EXERCISES

IDEA SHEET 9–8

Directions: Observe your friends. List all the different exercises children do naturally.

DATE	PERSON	EXERCISE

© 1992 by The Center for Applied Research in Education

EXERCISES

OPEN-ENDED IDEA SHEET

© 1992 by The Center for Applied Research in Education

"Over in the Meadow"
(Traditional Song)

Over in the meadow, in the sand, in the sun,
Lived an old mother toad and her little toadie one.
"Wink!" said the mother; "I wink," said the one:
So she winked and she blinked in the sand, in the sun.

Over in the meadow, where the stream runs so blue,
Lived an old mother fish and her little fishies two.
"Swim!" said the mother; "We swim," said the two:
So they swam and they leaped where the stream runs so blue.

Over in the meadow, in a hole in a tree,
Lived an old mother bluebird and her little birdies three.
"Sing!" said the mother; "We sing," said the three:
So they sang and were glad in the hole in the tree.

Over in the meadow, in the reeds on the shore,
Lived an old mother muskrat and her little muskies four.
"Dive!" said the mother; "We dive," said the four:
So they dived and they burrowed in the reeds on the shore.

Over in the meadow, in a snug beehive,
Lived an old mother honeybee with little honeys five.
"Buzz!" said the mother; "We buzz," said the five:
So they buzzed and they hummed in the snug beehive.

Over in the meadow, in a nest built of sticks,
Lived a black mother crow and her little crows six.
"Caw!" said the mother; "We caw," said the six:
So they cawed and they called in their nest built of sticks.

Over in the meadow, where the grass is so even,
Lived a gay mother cricket and her little crickets seven.
"Chirp!" said the mother; "We chirp," said the seven:
So they chirped cheery notes in the grass soft and even.

Over in the meadow, by the old mossy gate,
Lived a brown mother lizard and her little lizards eight.
"Bask!" said the mother; "We bask," said the eight:
So they basked in the sun, by the old mossy gate.

Over in the meadow, where the clear pools shine,
Lived a green mother frog and her little froggies nine.
"Croak!" said the mother; "We croak," said the nine:
So they croaked and they jumped, where the clear pools shine.

Over in the meadow, in a soft shady glen,
Lived a mother firefly and her little flies ten.
"Shine!" said the mother; "We shine," said the ten:
So they shone like stars, in the soft, shady glen.

MY ILLUSTRATION

© 1992 by The Center for Applied Research in Education

"Over in the Meadow"
Traditional Song

© 1992 by The Center for Applied Research in Education

"OVER IN THE MEADOW"
(Traditional Song)

Language Arts Teaching Activities
Skill: Verbs

- Cut out shapes of animals mentioned in the song and write the corresponding verb on the shape. What verbs can you add to the list? Share your list with a partner to get even more ideas.
- Compare the verbs and animals from the story on Idea Sheet 9-9. Which verbs are the most versatile?
- Create dramatic motions for the animals in the song. Can an audience guess which animal is being pantomimed?
- Evaluate the game. What would have made the presentations easier? Why? For example, different props, more time, audiovisual equipment, more people.

© 1992 by The Center for Applied Research in Education

Math Teaching Activities
Skill: Counting

- Sing the song with stick puppets. If everyone in the class makes puppets of all the animals, how many puppets would be made all together? If the class split into groups, how many puppets would be made?
- Plan to perform the song using Idea Sheet 9-10. How many minutes should be allotted per verse? How many minutes total does it take to perform? If groups move offstage after their verses, how many minutes does that take? What other "how many" questions can be generated?

- Create a scenic backdrop with a numerical pattern for the dramatization of the song.

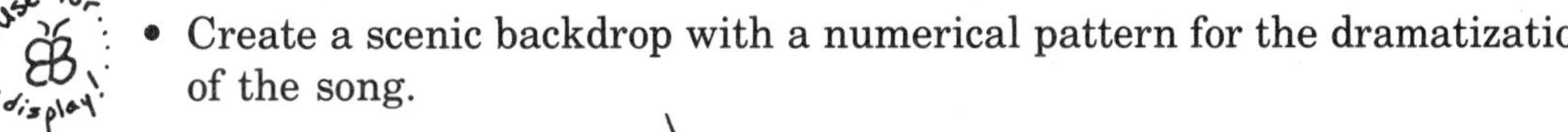

- Place the names of performers in a hat. Draw out one name and have everyone write a positive comment about the performer. Collect all the comments and read them aloud.

Social Studies Teaching Activities
Skill: Maps

- Collect many different kinds of maps and take time just to look at them (for example, a school map, geological survey map, road maps, or aerial maps).
- Using Idea Sheet 9–11, compare all the different maps. Which ones show features that apply to the song? What features are not included in the song?

- Create a map showing all the habitats of the animals in the song. Add appropriate details.
- Write supportive statements for the extra items and areas that you included on the map.

Science Teaching Activities
Skill: Habitats

- List words from the song that describe each habitat. What words can be added to each list?
- Use Ezra Jack Keats's book, *Over in the Meadow,* and other available pictures to analyze habitat pictures for human-made and natural features. For example,

feature	man-made	natural
meadow...		X
gate	X	
Stone wall	X	X
rocks		X

Web those features specific to meadows on Idea Sheet 9–12. Consider making webs for other habitats.

- Use two boxes stacked on top of each other to create a diorama of the habitat for each verse.

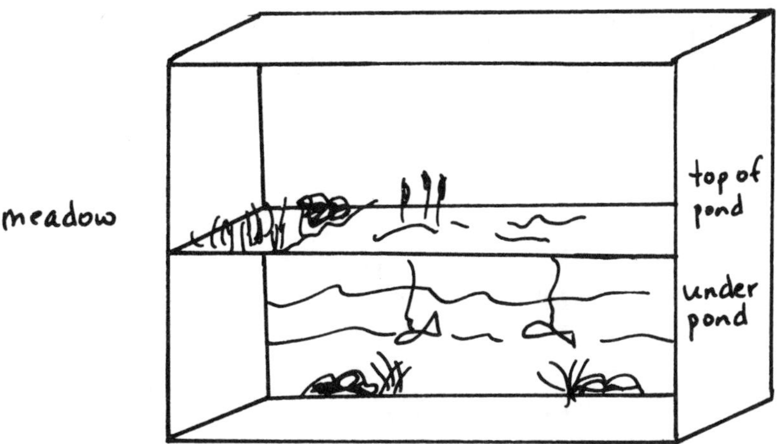

- Evaluate the dioramas. Which used natural materials? What human-made materials were useful in simulating natural features? Write your opinion of the best way to create a diorama.

Name ______________________

OVER IN THE MEADOW

IDEA SHEET 9–9

Directions: List animals and their actions mentioned in the song. Complete the grid by checking all the animals that can perform each action.

ANIMALS

VERBS/ACTIONS	bird								
sing									

© 1992 by The Center for Applied Research in Education

Name ______________________

OVER IN THE MEADOW

IDEA SHEET 9–10

Directions: Use this planning sheet to organize a performance of "Over in the Meadow."

WHAT NEEDS TO BE ORGANIZED?	WHO WILL DO IT?	WHEN DOES IT NEED TO BE DONE?	WHAT MATERIALS ARE NEEDED?
Time			
Puppets			
Scenery			
Props/instruments			
Posters/invitations			

© 1992 by The Center for Applied Research in Education

Name ______________________

OVER IN THE MEADOW

IDEA SHEET 9–11

Directions: List things from the song that are found in meadows. Compare your list with maps of meadows that you collect. (Local park services, chambers of commerce, and visitors' centers may have maps of areas that contain meadows.)

Use the back of this sheet to compose a new verse for the song that includes one of the features you have listed above.

© 1992 by The Center for Applied Research in Education

Name ____________________

OVER IN THE MEADOW

IDEA SHEET 9–12

Directions: Research to make a web of all the features of a meadow. Add ideas of your own that can be inferred from the poem and the research.

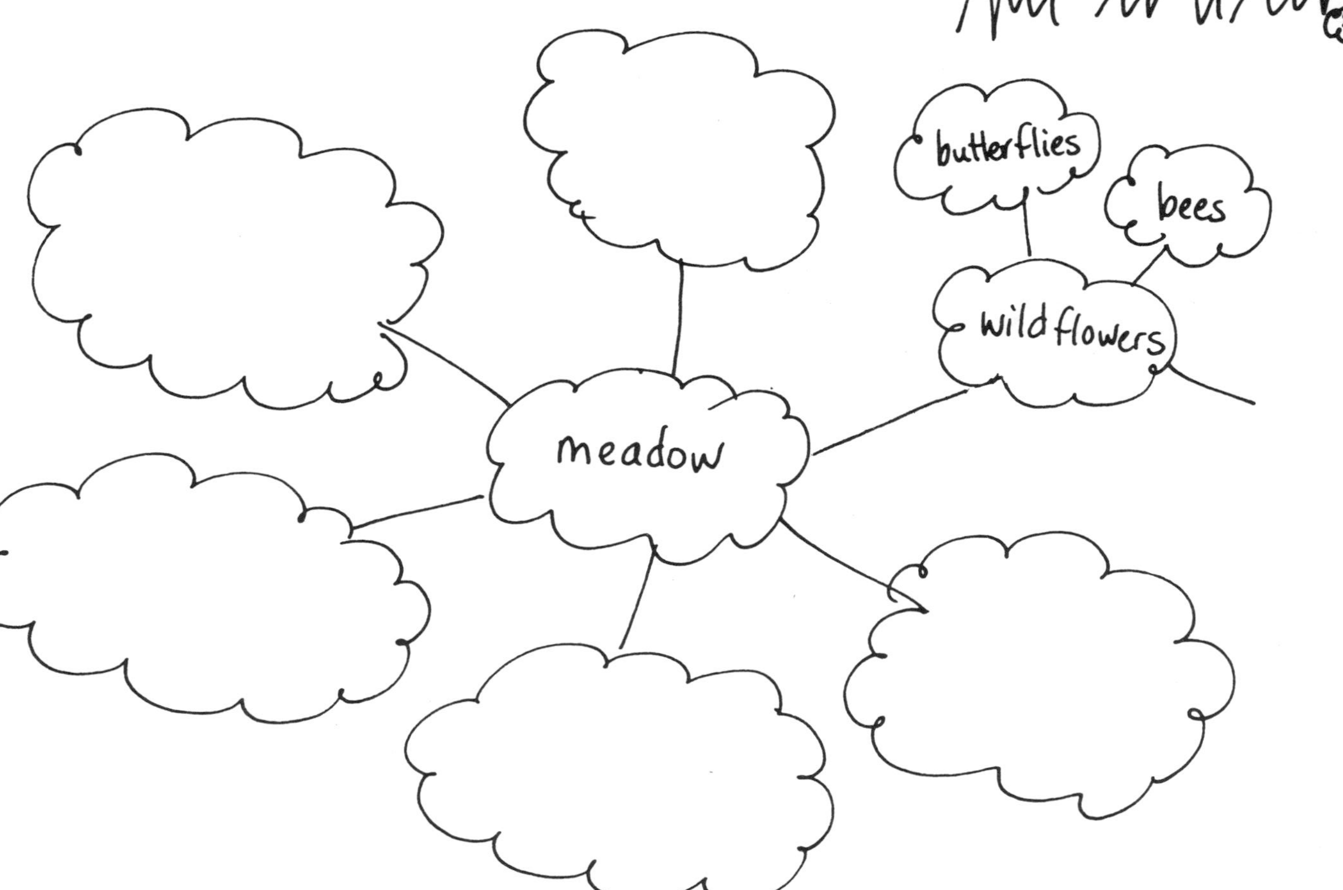

BONUS! Make a wall-sized web that incorporates everyone's ideas.

© 1992 by The Center for Applied Research in Education

OVER IN THE MEADOW

OPEN-ENDED IDEA SHEET

© 1992 by The Center for Applied Research in Education

10

June

SONG AND DANCE MAN
by Karen Ackerman
Illustrated by Stephen Gammell

(New York: Alfred A. Knopf, 1988)
Caldecott Award Winner, 1989

This story describes a special ritual shared by a grandpa and his three grandchildren. Climbing steep, wooden steps to an attic where his vaudeville trunk is stored, Grandpa puts on his tap shoes and revisits the days of being a song and dance man. The children lovingly admire his talents, wishing they could have seen him in the good old days. Grandpa enjoys his special memories but assures the children that he treasures the times with his grandchildren even more.

Language Arts Teaching Activities
Skill: Vocabulary Development

- Make a dictionary of interesting vocabulary words from the story (for example, *vaudeville, bowler hats, top hats, leather trimmed trunk, corns, shammy cloth, spotlight, show time, old soft shoe, slippery sounds, tin roof, canyon echo,* and *grand finale*).
- List the descriptive phrases the author uses; read the story without those descriptions, and then read it with them. Compare. What conclusions can be made about the use of descriptive phrases?

- In what other directions might the ending of the story go? The author wonders how much Grandpa really misses the good old days. What else might Grandpa be thinking? Draw a picture of Grandpa, with possible thoughts listed around him.
- Consider how Grandpa enjoyed using things from his past that held special memories for him. Spend time in the classroom having students survey each other about special memories. Use Idea Sheet 10–1 to record ideas. Have a sharing day during which children show something from their past (or their family's past) that has special meaning.
- Evaluate different family rituals. The shared attic time between Grandpa and the children is something they've enjoyed many times. Why is it so much fun? Encourage children to share family or school rituals and describe why they are important.

Math Teaching Activities
Skill: Patterns

- Identify various patterns that are fun to tap while sitting or standing. Work from a single tap up to what the author describes as "a woodpecker on a tree." Have tap exercise breaks during the school day. Take the patterning one step further and consider the pattern of the vaudeville show: Dance–magic–sing–joke–pause. Act out Grandpa's pattern.
- Invite a tap dancer to class and try to analyze the tap patterns. Or play a variety of music and deduce which music suits a slow tap pattern, which suits a fast pattern. Collect objects that make a tapping sound. Use the music for class tap exercise breaks.
- Think of all the kinds of shows that have grand finales (for example, fireworks, orchestra, or animals). Create a tap pattern that would be a grand finale.
- Judge the grand finale patterns using Idea Sheet 10–2. What criteria is appropriate for grand finales performed onstage? Create a judging form, and have the top five patterns performed for the class.

Social Studies Teaching Activities
Skill: Memories

- Key into the three phrases "good old days," "time before TV days," and "song and dance days" and record things Grandpa enjoyed "digging out" on Idea Sheet 10–3. Have children interview an adult or grandparent about their early memories, and add their favorite items to the worksheet.

- In a chart, compile major points from the memories interviews explained above. Compare and contrast the information. Does geographic location or age play into the person's response?

- Have children write what they think they will share with their grandchildren as memories from "the good old days."
- Discuss how memory can be selective. Survey classmates for their prominent memories. What conclusions can be drawn?

Science Teaching Activities
Skill: Senses

- The author appeals to all the senses in the descriptive text. List examples from the story on Idea Sheet 10–4.
- Play different musical pieces and have children classify the selections. What music is suitable for tap dancing, for quiet listening, or for work time? Incorporate some of the selections into different periods of the school day.

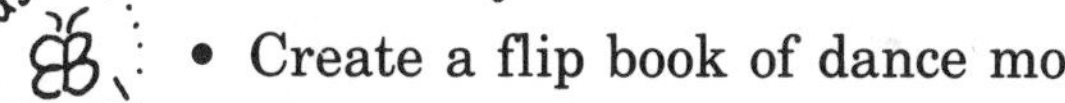

- Create a flip book of dance motion.
- Extend the flip books into a study of color and sound. Produce them both in color and black and white. Flip them with and without a musical background. Collect viewers' reactions and evaluate. How does incorporating more senses affect people's opinions of the flip book?

Name ______________________

SONG AND DANCE MAN

IDEA SHEET 10–1

Directions: Make a list of kinds of memories (earliest, happiest, . . .). Survey three classmates to find out about their memories. Record the information on the hat chart. Then write any conclusions you can draw on the hat brim OR graph the information on the back of this sheet.

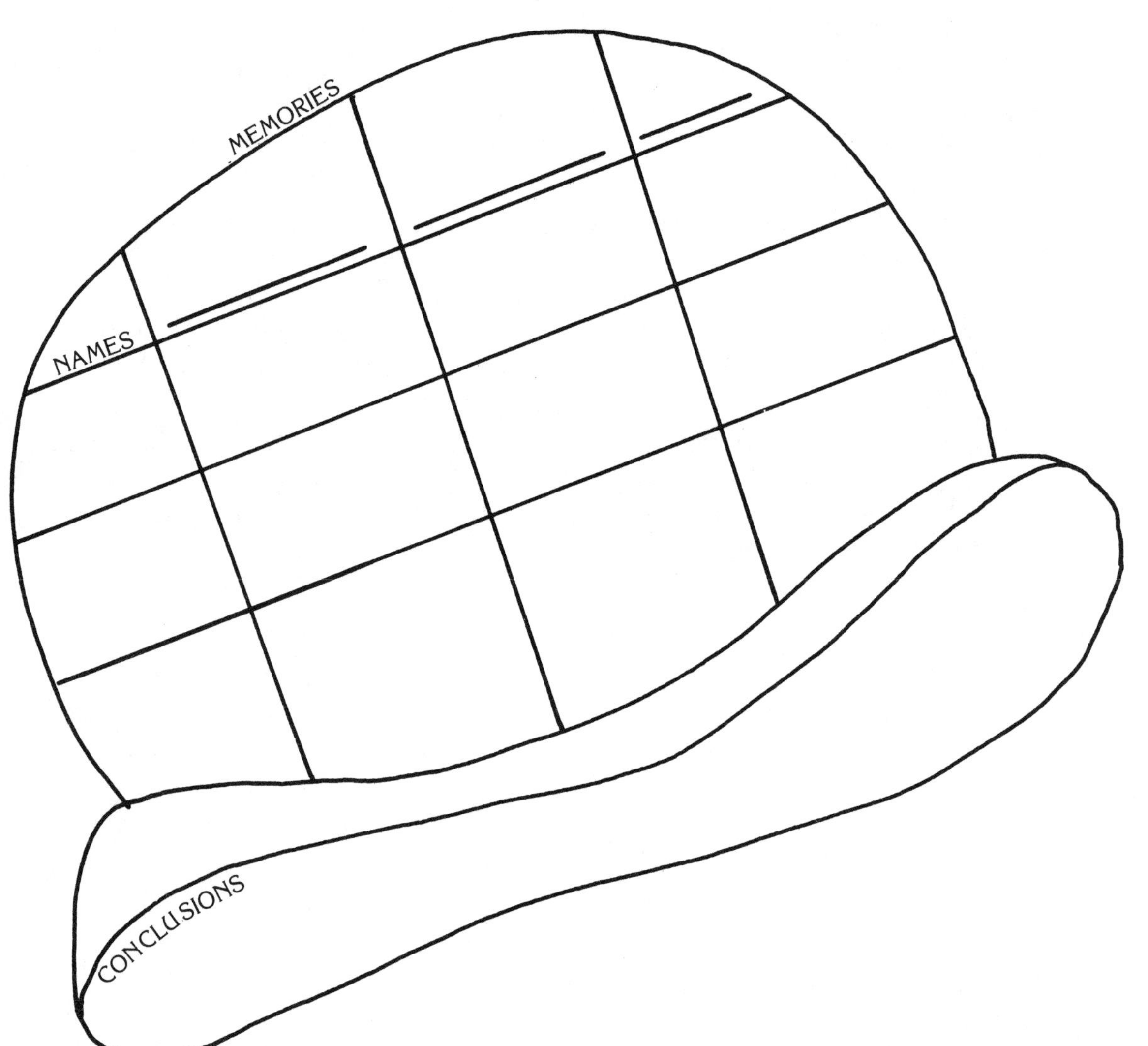

© 1992 by The Center for Applied Research in Education

Name ______________________

SONG AND DANCE MAN

IDEA SHEET 10–2

Directions: Have different class members perform tapping patterns. Evaluate each tapping pattern by circling words that describe it and completing the response form. Use blanks to add other criteria or adjectives that occur to you.

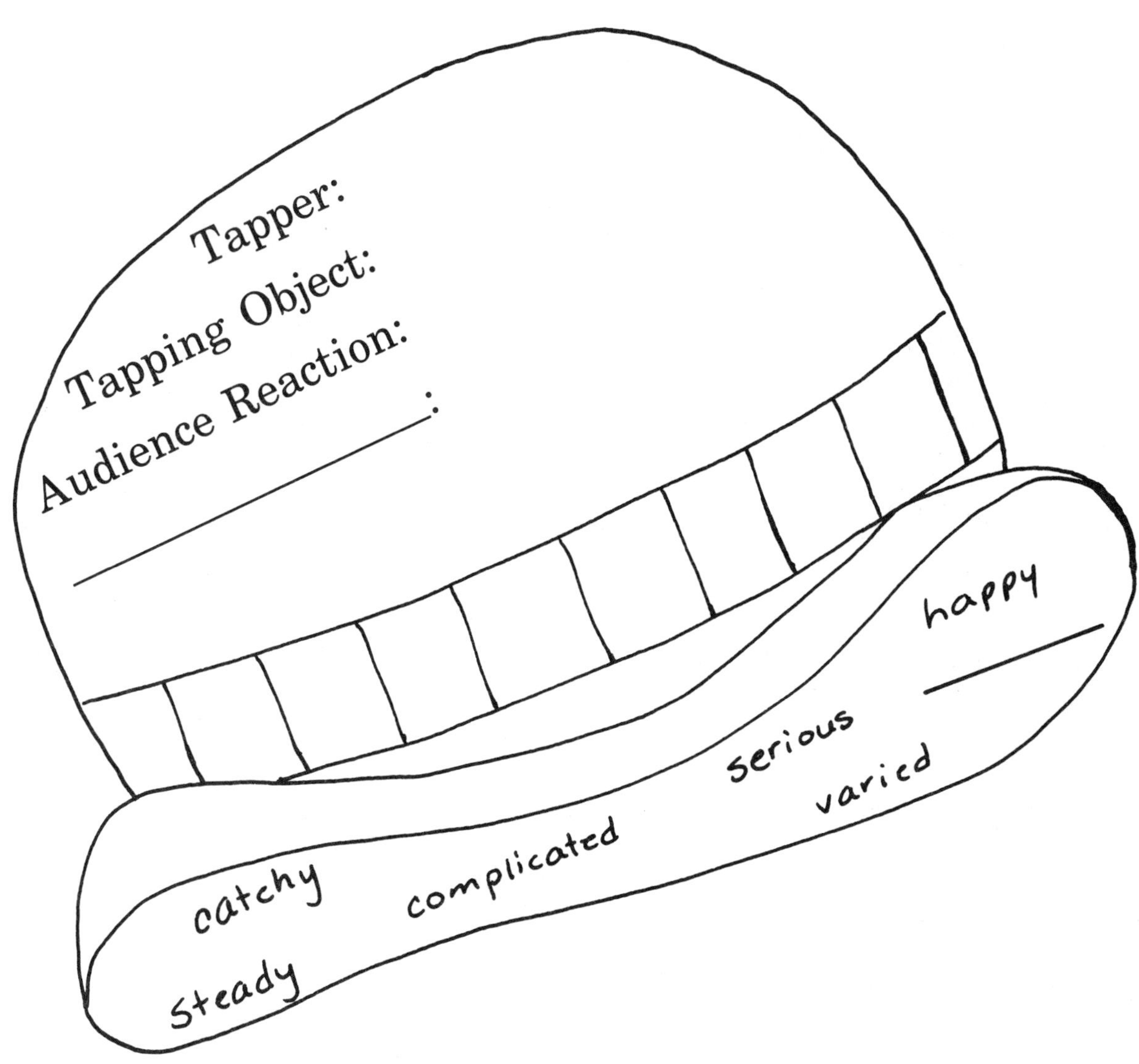

© 1992 by The Center for Applied Research in Education

Name ____________________

SONG AND DANCE MAN

IDEA SHEET 10–3

Directions: On the hat, write things from the past that Grandpa enjoyed "digging out" once in a while. In the space outside the hat, write things people in your family like to look at occasionally.

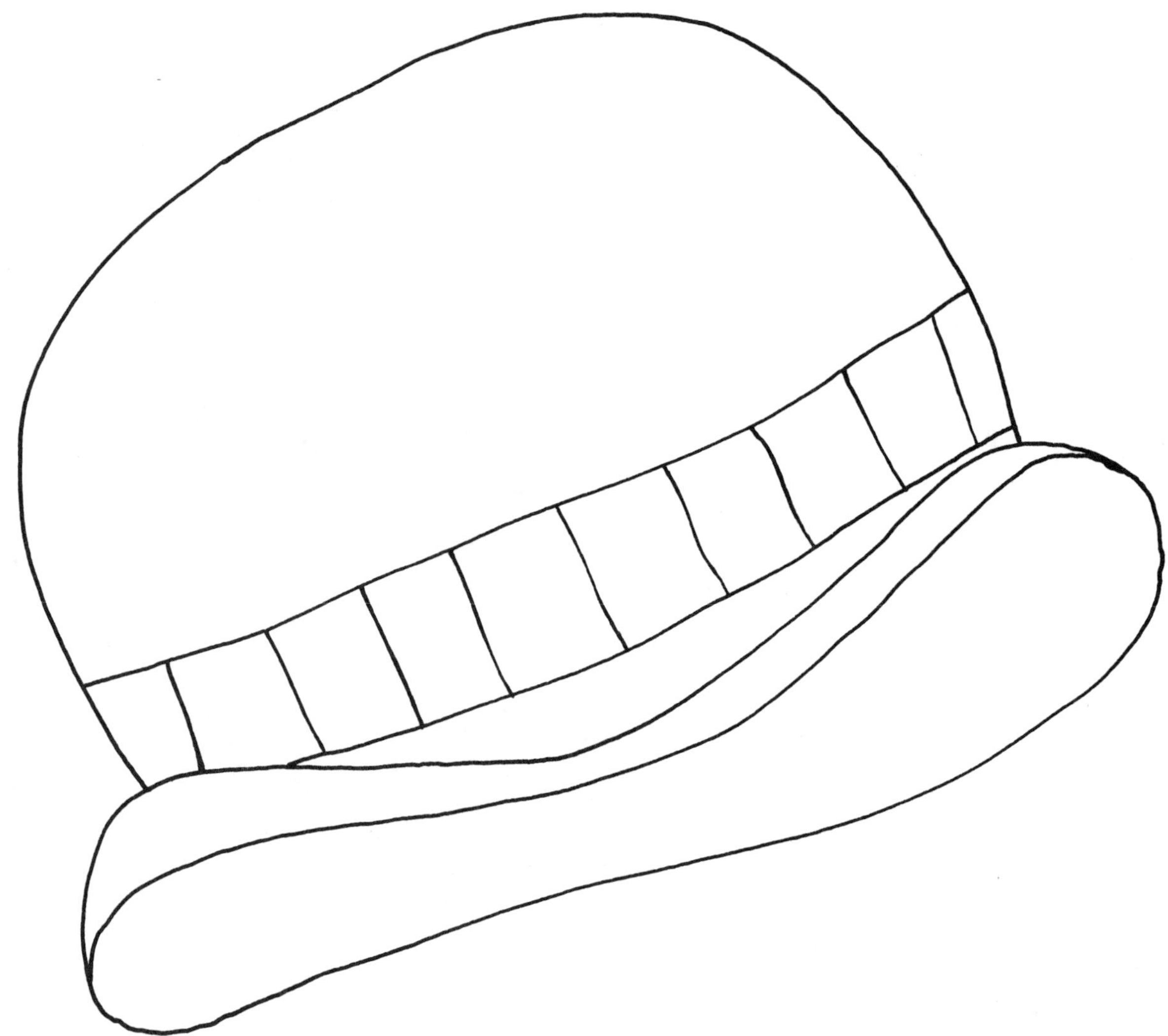

Name ______________________

SONG AND DANCE MAN

IDEA SHEET 10–4

Directions: Cut out five hat patterns, one for each of the five senses. Write the sense on the hat band. List examples in the story on other parts of the hat. Staple the hats together to make a resource for *your* writing.

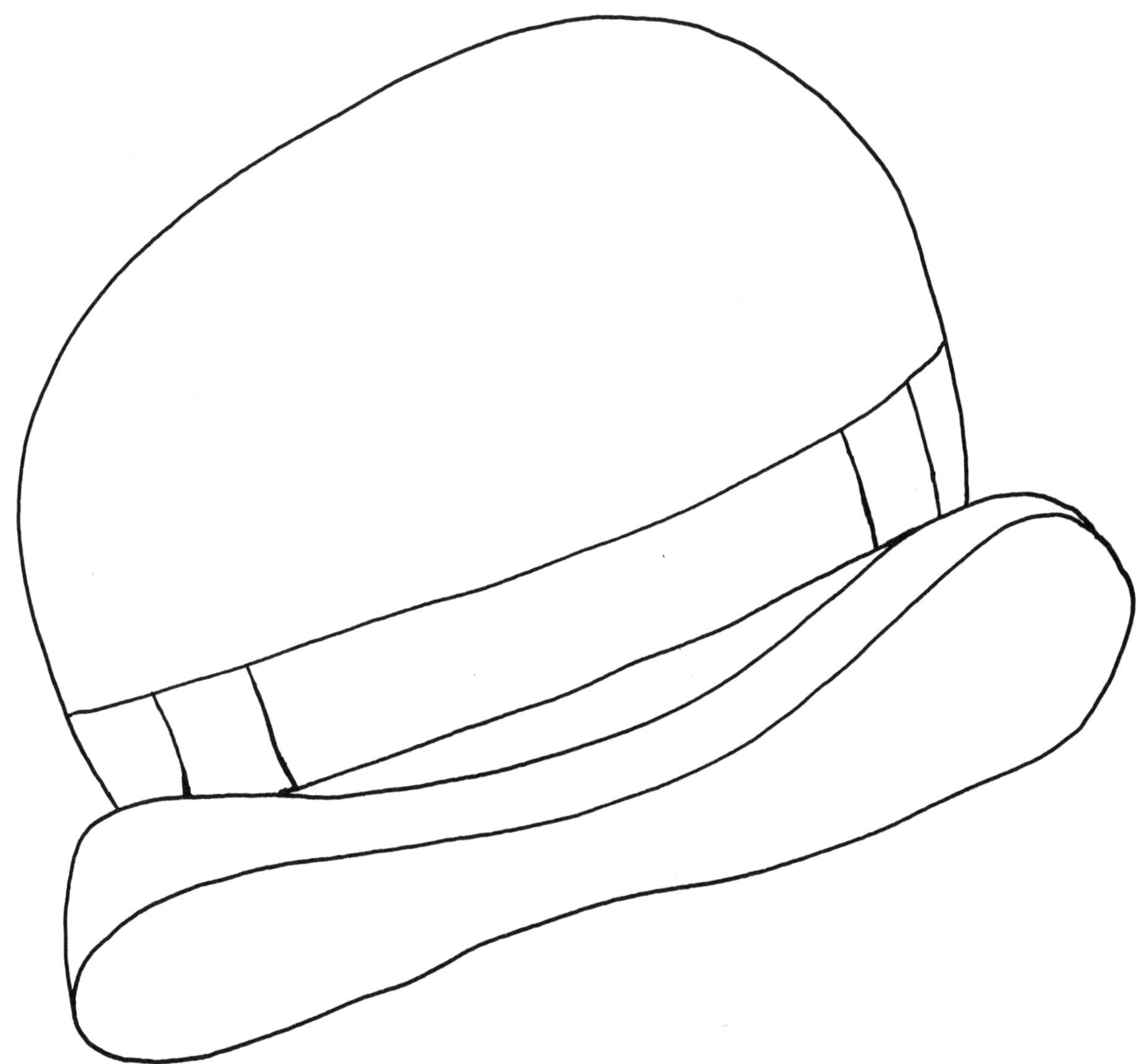

CHALLENGE! Can you write a story that appeals to each of the five senses? Use the hat booklet to help.

SONG AND DANCE MAN *OPEN-ENDED IDEA SHEET*

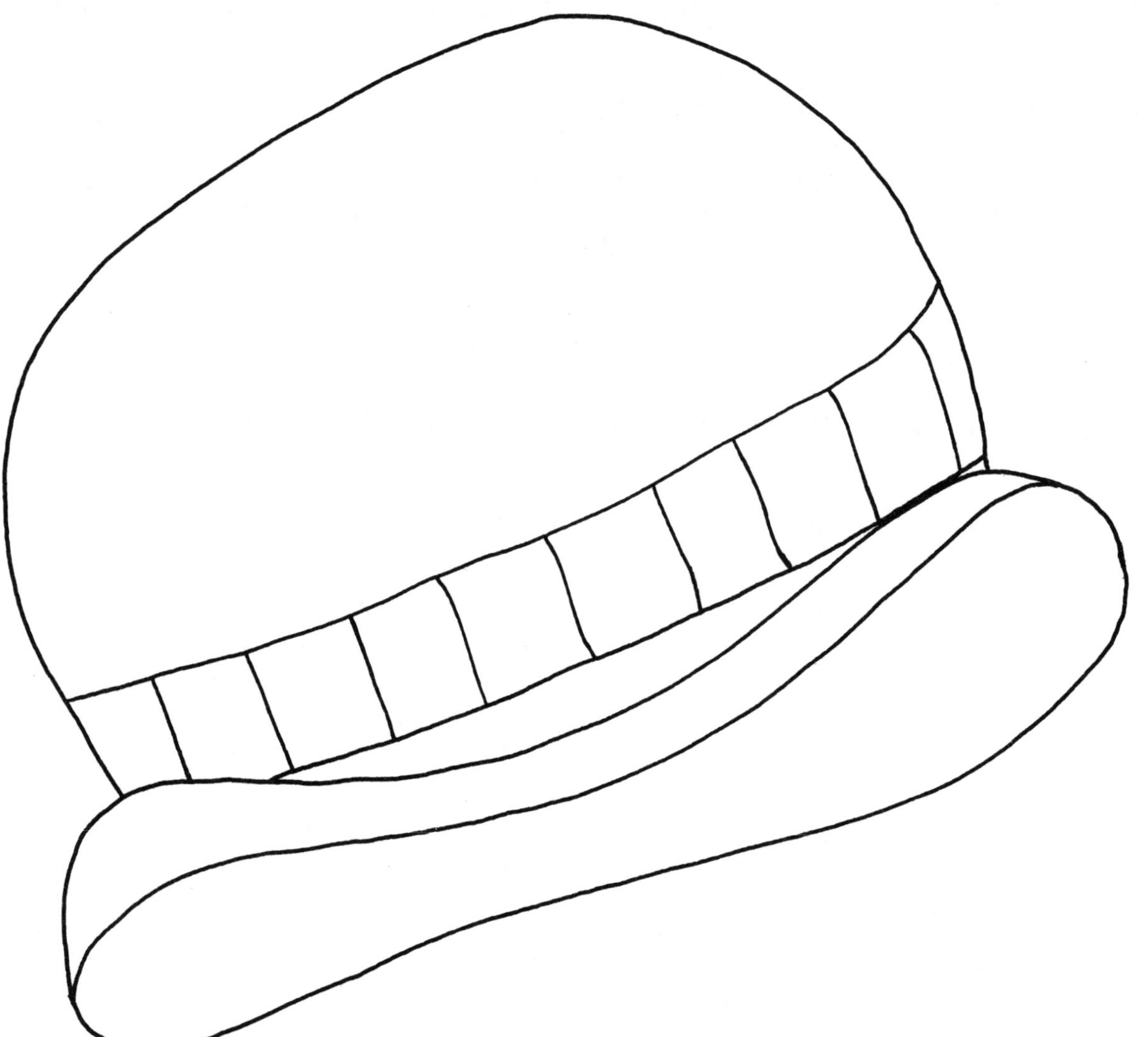

© 1992 by The Center for Applied Research in Education

"Hector the Collector"
by Shel Silverstein

Hector the Collector
Collected bits of string,
Collected dolls with broken heads
And rusty bells that would not ring.
Pieces out of picture puzzles,
Bent-up nails and ice-cream sticks,
Twists of wires, worn-out tires,
Paper bags and broken bricks.
Old chipped vases, half shoelaces,
Gatlin' guns that wouldn't shoot,
Leaky boats that wouldn't float
And stopped-up horns that wouldn't toot.
Butter knives that had no handles,
Copper keys that fit no locks,
Rings that were too small for fingers,
Dried-up leaves and patched-up socks.
Worn-out belts that had no buckles,
'Lectric trains that had no tracks,
Airplane models, broken bottles,
Three-legged chairs and cups with cracks.
Hector the Collector
Loved these things with all his soul–
Loved them more than shining diamonds,
Loved them more than glistenin' gold.
Hector called to all the people,
"Come and share my treasure trunk!"
And all the silly sightless people
Came and looked . . . and called it junk.

MY ILLUSTRATION

© 1992 by The Center for Applied Research in Education

"HECTOR THE COLLECTOR"
by Shel Silverstein
from Where the Sidewalk Ends

(New York: Harper and Row, 1974)

Language Arts Teaching Activities
Skill: Application

- Divide the class into groups. Ask each group to devise motions for different parts of the poem. Choral read the poem, with groups performing their motions.
- Why does the name Hector the Collector attract your attention? Look in the phone book for examples of business names that capitalize on ending sounds or alliteration. List them on Idea Sheet 10–5. Draw conclusions about how to name a business.

- Compose poems for the following jobs using the same writing format as Hector the Collector.
  - Board Washer
  - Messenger
  - Litterbug Patrol
  - Closet Checker
  - Line Leader
  - Plant Tender

  For example,

  Peter the Board Washer
  Washed the board every night;
  He left streaks on the board
  That created quite a fright!

- Evaluate the job poems. Are they humorous? catchy? silly? convincing? Explain your opinion with supporting statements.

Math Teaching Activities
Skills: Collection, Classification

- Collect all the stuff Hector the Collector considers valuable.
- Categorize Hector's things by attributes on Idea Sheet 10–6.
- What are all the uses for __________ (items from the poem)? Write a class book.

- Evaluate ideas from the previous activity. Complete this sentence:

  A ____________ would be useful because ______________________________

  ____.

Social Studies Teaching Activities
Skill: Cooperation

- Discuss reasons why one person's junk is another person's treasure. Cite examples such as yard sales, thrift shops, white elephant parties (exchange used items rather than new gifts), etc.
- Use the classified ads to categorize the types of items people include in yard sales.
- Plan a white elephant class party.
- Use Idea Sheet 10–7 to evaluate how Hector felt throughout the poem. What could people have done to make Hector feel good at the end of the poem? Compare Hector's possible reactions to ridicule and to support. Which would you offer Hector? Why?

Science Teaching Activities
Skill: Recycling

- Find out about recycling in your area. Put the information in a flyer to display in your school office.
- Recheck Hector's collections. What things do you and Hector recycle? Keep a week-long log of things you recycle using Idea Sheet 10–8. What would you include on a suggested list of recyclables for your friends?

- Create something frivolous or useful out of nonrecyclable materials.
- Write "kid suggestions" for recycling in your classroom, school, or community. Editorialize about why it's important to help solve the current waste problems. Share your opinions with an adult.

Name ____________________

HECTOR THE COLLECTOR

IDEA SHEET 10–5

Directions: Use a telephone book or other resource to search for businesses whose names use alliteration or catchy ending sounds. List them on the chart.

ALLITERATION	CATCHY ENDING SOUNDS
Cozy Kitchen Candy	Hector the Collector

This activity was ____________________
(difficult or easy)

because ____________________

____________________.

© 1992 by The Center for Applied Research in Education

Name ___________________________

HECTOR THE COLLECTOR

IDEA SHEET 10–6

Directions: Think of two attributes that fit many of Hector's things. Use a Venn diagram to classify the items. If you have used a Venn diagram before, add a third circle.

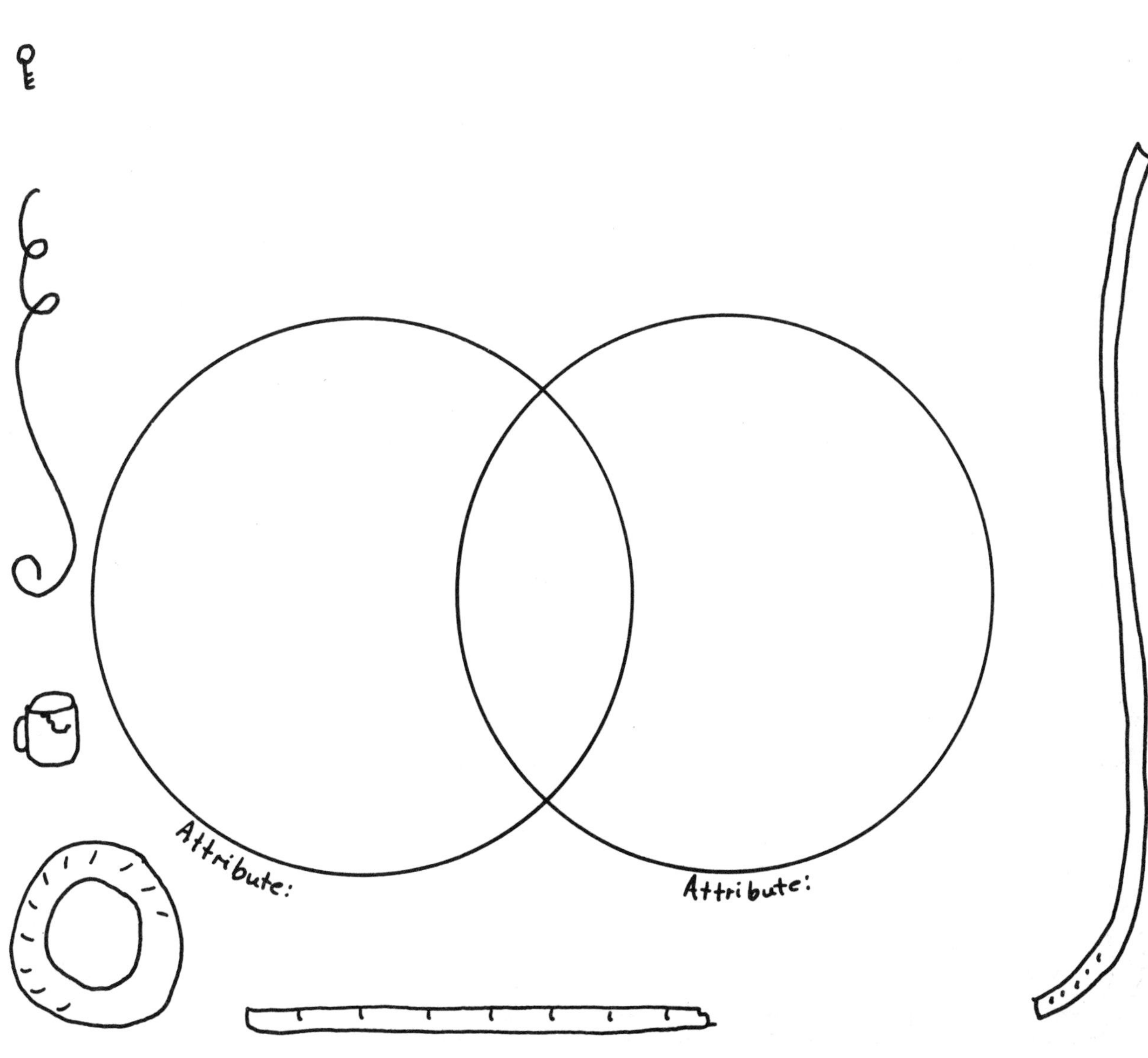

© 1992 by The Center for Applied Research in Education

Name ____________________

HECTOR THE COLLECTOR

IDEA SHEET 10–7

Directions: Explore the author's message by comparing two possible endings to the poem. List your ideas of how Hector feels and what he does in response to the people's different reactions. After you have completed the chart, turn over this sheet and write about what might have given Shel Silverstein the idea for this poem.

If the poem ends: Hector called to all the people "Come and share my treasure _____! And all the friendly caring people Came and looked and called it _____.	If the poem ends: Hector called to all the people ______________________ ______________________ ______________________
Hector will feel:	Hector will feel:
Hector will (action):	Hector will (action):

© 1992 by The Center for Applied Research in Education

Name ____________________

HECTOR THE COLLECTOR

IDEA SHEET 10–8

Directions: Keep a log of things you throw away each day of the week.

	ITEM	POSSIBLE USES
S	Soup can	Sand mold, telephone...
M		
T		
W		
Th		
F		
S		

© 1992 by The Center for Applied Research in Education

HECTOR THE COLLECTOR

OPEN-ENDED IDEA SHEET

© 1992 by The Center for Applied Research in Education

"Jamaica Farewell"
(Traditional Song)

Down the way where the nights are gay,
And the sun shines brightly on the mountaintop,
I took a trip on a sailing ship,
And when I reached Jamaica I made a stop.

Chorus

But I'm sad to say, I'm on my way,
Won't be back for many a day,
My heart is down, my head is turning around,
I miss all my friends in Kingstontown.

Down at the market you can hear,
All the ladies cry out while on their heads they bear,
Akie rice, salt fish are nice,
And the sun is fine any time of the year.

Chorus

Sounds of laughter everywhere,
And the children sway to and fro,
I must declare that my heart is there,
Though I've been from Maine to Mexico.

Chorus (twice)

MY ILLUSTRATION

© 1992 by The Center for Applied Research in Education

"Jamaica Farewell"
Traditional Song

© 1992 by The Center for Applied Research in Education

"JAMAICA FAREWELL"
(Traditional Song)

Language Arts Teaching Activities
Skill: Calypso Music

- Collect examples of calypso music and enjoy listening to it.
- Research calypso music. What is unique about it?
- Use rhythm instruments to play a calypso beat. Make up school chants to accompany the instruments.
- Use Idea Sheet 10–9 to consider three elements of calypso music: rhythm, tune, and lyrics. How does each make you feel? Which do you pay attention to first? Why? In your opinion, which is most important and why?

Math Teaching Activities
Skill: Measurement (Mileage, Time, and Temperature)

- Identify the measurements relating to the song on Idea Sheet 10–10. What mile measurements can be determined? How much time is mentioned in the song? What temperatures can be inferred?
- Look through travel brochures of Jamaica. What mathematical facts do they include? Determine the distance from your school to Jamaica, and compare it with other vacation spots. Chart your findings.

- Create an advertising poster for one of the vacation spots and include mathematical facts on it.
- What math facts would convince people to travel to Jamaica? Why?

Social Studies Teaching Activities
Skill: Jamaica

- Orient yourself to Jamaica. Collect travel brochures and gather information from the library.
- Compare the various travel brochures. Categorize the information they contain. Identify lines from the song that correspond to the brochure information.
- Use the brochure information to add to the song.
- Use Idea Sheet 10–11 to compare Jamaica with your area. Which aspects of each place do you prefer? Why?

Science Teaching Activities
Skill: The Sun, Seasons

- Use Idea Sheet 10–12 to explain why the words "the sun is fine any time of year" are true of Jamaica. Include facts about the earth's rotation in your explanation.
- Have students write a log entry in a science journal explaining the rotation of the earth. Include examples of how the rotation affects different parts of globe.

- Paint a mural showing the different activities of the song. Make the sun the central focus of the mural.
- What other places and things are dependent on the sun throughout the year? Explain why each depends on the sun.

Name ______________________

JAMAICA FAREWELL

IDEA SHEET 10–9

Directions: Listen to several calypso songs. Complete the chart by writing comments stating your opinions of the rhythm, tune, and lyrics of each song.

In your opinion, which elements are most important? Why? Explain your ideas on the back of this sheet.

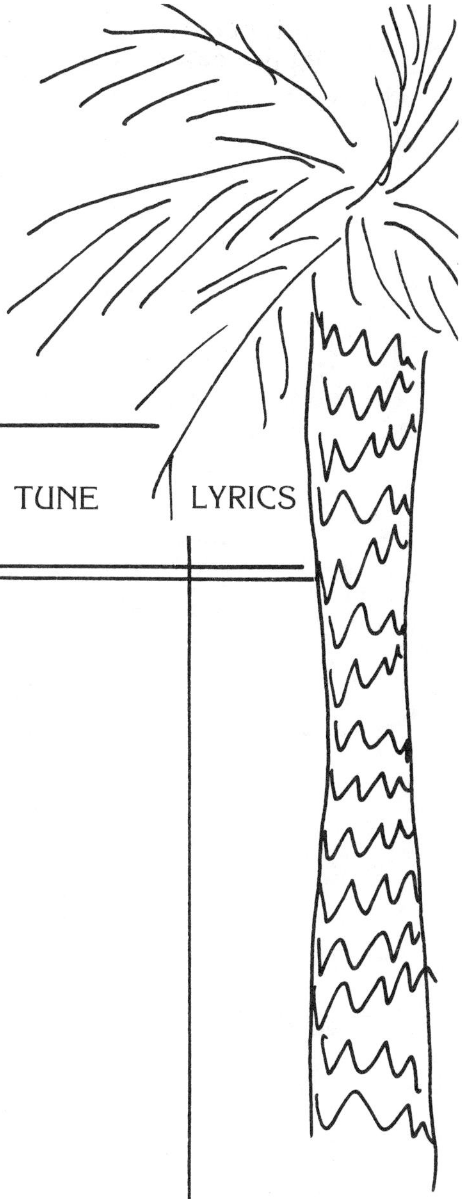

SONG TITLE	RHYTHM	TUNE	LYRICS
"Jamaica Farewell"			

© 1992 by The Center for Applied Research in Education

Name ______________________

JAMAICA FAREWELL

IDEA SHEET 10–10

Directions: Collect measurement facts about Jamaica. Record them on the appropriate hat shapes.

distance

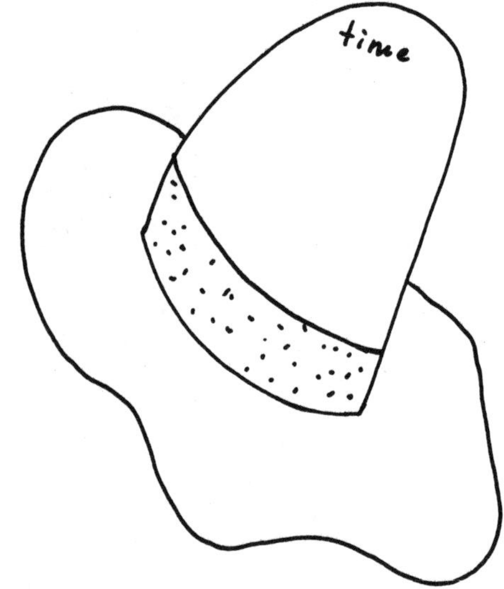

temperature

CREATIVE CHALLENGE! Use the math facts to create a travel poster to attract travelers.

© 1992 by The Center for Applied Research in Education

Name ______________________

JAMAICA FAREWELL

IDEA SHEET 10–11

Directions: Compare Jamaica to your area by completing the Venn diagram.

Use a highlighting marker to indicate the best features of each place. Be ready to tell the class why you believe these to be true.

© 1992 by The Center for Applied Research in Education

Name ______________________________

JAMAICA FAREWELL

IDEA SHEET 10–12

Directions: In your own words, explain why "the sun is fine any time of year" in Jamaica.

Share your explanation with a friend. Revise your explanation to adjust to questions he or she may have.

© 1992 by The Center for Applied Research in Education

JAMAICA FAREWELL

OPEN-ENDED IDEA SHEET

© 1992 by The Center for Applied Research in Education

A personal view from Donna . . .

I have spent years teaching children to read through almost every method you can imagine, and children *have* learned to read. I'm enough of a realist, however, to have observed that many children have actually learned to read in spite of my well-intentioned methods.

In 1986, the teachers at my school were encouraged to experiment with a whole language approach to language arts instruction. I made small changes at first, but the positive results convinced me to make bolder moves. Whole language learning makes sense to me and to my students. Children naturally learn to read, write, speak, and listen by doing those things at school—and they get better at them because they enjoy working at them.

When discussing whole language teaching, I am often asked, "What are you doing that's different?" My reply can range from explaining the daily classroom routine to sharing what I've learned about how young children learn best. My language arts plans have been transformed from following directions in a basal teacher's manual to really *planning* integrated learning experiences. It's a little trickier, but it's also more interesting and definitely more rewarding in terms of student response.

The framework I use to create my plans is simple. Every day,

- I read aloud to the class.
- The students and I read together (big books, poetry, posters, song lyrics, etc.).
- The students and I read and write independently.
- The students have some opportunity to share their reading, writing, and thinking with others.
- The students are involved in some kind of "hook" activity. This can be an art or science project, a creative book extension, a special assembly, a guest speaker, a film, a game—something that lures kids into learning.

Several times a week,

- I model writing.
- I teach a specific skill (mini-lesson).

- I listen to each child read.
- I observe each child's writing.
- I conference with each child.

I love teaching through the whole language approach because every child succeeds at his or her own rate and every day is unique. Assessment focuses on the positive–what each child is able to do, what progress he or she is making. Parents are thrilled that their children enjoy reading and writing and thinking about literature. I'm delighted to be able to incorporate the "real world" into daily learning rather than viewing special events as interruptions.

In short, the whole language approach enables students to learn to make sense of the exciting world of print.

Donna

A personal view from Margie . . .

My teaching roles have varied throughout my years in elementary schools. I've taught in open and self-contained classrooms. I've enjoyed self-contained arrangements, team teaching, and resource teaching. It's been delightful both to implement and observe diverse teaching practices, and it continues to be so! As whole language has come to the educational forum, it seems to be following the wide spectrum of implementation that other educational themes have been subjected to. Whatever your philosophical stand with regard to whole language and educational themes, there seem to be core teaching practices involving reading, writing, and speaking that consistently promote student success. Some of my observations through the years include the following.

Independent daily writing time is something all students–kindergarten and up–find an enjoyable learning activity. Some teachers give a starting sentence, others pose an idea, and some leave the topic completely up to the child. All children record ideas in some fashion. The kindergartener may string letters together with a picture, a third grader may compose a paragraph, and a fifth grader may make a long list. Whatever the level of the response, all children find pleasure and pride in writing something of personal value and having the opportunity to share it. The writing is not perfect; children value the opportunity to write purely as a means of expression.

Diverse daily reading opportunities carry importance, too. Children read both self-selected books and teacher-chosen selections aloud in a group, with a grade level buddy, in a silent sustained reading time, over the school intercom, with a student tutor, with a parent volunteer, with a specialist, and with the principal. In every situation, the child is pleased to have someone actively listening to him or her read. The variety of sharing activities is what keeps interest and enthusiasm high.

Many children clamor for the opportunity to speak in front of a group or take a part in a play. Creative dramatics and "safe" speaking opportunities further enhance children's development. Even the shyest child stands in front of the room for show-and-tell when the classroom community conveys that everyone's contribution is necessary and valuable. It is essential to vary speaking opportunities and offer choices in order to match each child with preferred sharing opportunities.

It seems that classrooms oriented to learning experiences focused on children's needs flourish with creative energetic activity. Even the children themselves generate activity suggestions. A group working on a research project might divide up and have some students read and record information, others outline key points, and others draw posters illustrating important elements of the assigned topic. The teacher assumes the role of facilitating and guiding learning.

The challenge is to create a harmony between the teacher's skills and the students' abilities and interests. All of us know the "feel" of that harmony–it's what makes us teachers! Whole language is the very real opportunity to synthesize a variety of teaching practices with the needs of the learner. Through reading, writing, speaking, and listening opportunities that are integrated rather than broken into bits, children naturally put to use real-life learning skills. My greatest joy as a teacher is to foster life-long learning in the children with whom I work. Diverse yet purposeful teaching practices energize children. I hope the ideas in this book are useful in this sense.

DISCARD
KINSMAN FREE PUBLIC LIBRARY
6420 CHURCH ST.
BOX E
KINSMAN, OHIO 44428